SUCCESSFUL NEIGHBOURHOODS:
A GOOD PRACTICE GUIDE

PETE DUNCAN
AND SALLY THOMAS
SOCIAL REGENERATION CONSULTANTS

PUBLISHED BY THE
CHARTERED INSTITUTE OF HOUSING
AND THE HOUSING CORPORATION

The Chartered Institute of Housing

The Chartered Institute of Housing is the professional organisation for people who work in housing. Its purpose is to maximise the contribution housing professionals make to the wellbeing of communities. The Chartered Institute has over 20,000 members across the UK and the Asian Pacific working in a range of organisations – including housing associations, local authorities, arms length management organisations, the private sector and educational institutions.

Chartered Institute of Housing
Octavia House, Westwood Way
Coventry CV4 8JP
Telephone: 024 7685 1700
www.cih.org

The Housing Corporation

The Housing Corporation is the government agency which registers, regulates and funds over 1,500 social landlords in England which between them provide 2 million homes. The Corporation has an important role as a promoter of good practice in the social housing sector.

The Housing Corporation
149 Tottenham Court Road
London W1T 7BN
Tel: 020 7393 2000 Fax: 020 7393 2111
Website: http://www.housingcorp.gov.uk

Successful Neighbourhoods: a good practice guide
Written by Pete Duncan and Sally Thomas
Editor: Jane Allanson

© Chartered Institute of Housing and the Housing Corporation 2007
ISBN 978-1-905018-28-4

Graphic design by Jeremy Spencer
Cover photograph by Pete Duncan

Contents

Foreword by Rt Hon Ruth Kelly MP, Secretary of State for Communities
and Local Government and Minister for Women   **5**

About the Authors   **7**

Acknowledgements   **8**

Chapter 1	**Introduction**	**9**
	About this guide	9
	What is a neighbourhood?	10
	Managing neighbourhoods	11
	Who is the guide for?	12
Chapter 2	**Neighbourhoods: The Policy Context**	**14**
	Devolution – a changing landscape	14
	The government's modernisation agenda	15
	Narrowing the gap – tackling social exclusion	17
	Regional devolution	18
	The changing role of local government	18
	Local Area Agreements	20
	New roles for service providers	20
	From decent homes to mixed, sustainable communities: the implications for housing providers	21
Chapter 3	**The Neighbourhood Agenda**	**24**
	Devolving power and responsibility to the neighbourhood	25
	Strengthening neighbourhood governance	27
	Community asset ownership	31
	Gearing up for the new agenda – the implications for housing providers	33
Chapter 4	**What Makes a Successful Neighbourhood?**	**37**
	The lessons of history	38
	Why some neighbourhoods fail	40
	Successful neighbourhoods – the main factors	46
	How successful neighbourhoods can sustain themselves	51
Chapter 5	**Making It Happen: Neighbourhood Management**	**53**
	Neighbourhood management – the essential elements	54
	The pathfinder experience	57

	Mainstreaming neighbourhood management	60
	Setting up a delivery body	65
	How to create and sustain successful neighbourhood partnerships	67
	The changing role of local councillors	71
	The importance of cultural change	72
	A success story: neighbourhood policing	73
	Neighbourhood management: narrowing the gap	75
	Bringing together physical, social and economic renewal	77
	Setting new standards for service providers	80
	Strengthening the housing provider's role	81
Chapter 6	**Local Communities: In the Driving Seat?**	**85**
	Community engagement: making it happen	86
	How involved are local communities in their neighbourhoods?	99
	Taking more control	101
	Community asset ownership	103
Chapter 7	**Putting It into Practice – What Should Housing Providers Do?**	**111**
	The business case for the neighbourhood agenda	111
	Resourcing the neighbourhood	118
	Rationalising the neighbourhood housing stock	122
	Changing mono-tenure areas	123
	Choice-based lettings	125
	Supporting stronger, more cohesive communities	126
	Delivering the Respect agenda	127
	Gearing up for change	128
	Evaluating impacts and outcomes	130
Chapter 8	**Looking Forward**	**136**
	A wider role for housing associations	137
	ALMOs – a new future for council housing?	138
	Towards the accountable neighbourhood	138
	Changing cultures, changing places	140
Appendices		
Appendix A	References and Sources of Further Information	143
Appendix B	Glossary	155
Appendix C	*Together We Can* Guide Neighbourhoods	158

Foreword

A message from Rt Hon Ruth Kelly MP, Secretary of State for Communities and Local Government and Minister for Women

This Government has an ambitious vision: to ensure that no-one is disadvantaged by where they live. To bring prosperity and opportunity to every community.

Achieving this vision means different actions at different levels – from the national, to the regional, to the local. Sometimes it can mean working right down at the level of individual neighbourhoods. It is often here that pockets of the most stubborn social and economic problems are encountered – from crime, to anti-social behaviour, to patterns of worklessness. Yet it is also here that the most ingenious and effective solutions are found, bringing public services together to meet people's needs and helping communities rediscover a sense of pride and purpose.

Over the past ten years many of this Government's successful regeneration programmes have focused on neighbourhood management. Initiatives like Neighbourhood Management Pathfinders and New Deal for Communities – along with a plethora of locally developed arrangements – have made a real difference for residents, not just by improving services but by giving people a bigger stake in the places where they live.

This guide brings together some of the best examples of what has been achieved. The variety of approaches is impressive.

Take Greater Lever in Bolton. The "Safe and Clean Charter", based on local people's priorities, sets out agreed targets for service providers to tackle crime and grime. The Charter has helped cut burglary and street litter, and there has been a significant increase in the number of people who like living in the area.

Take Community Counts in Gloucester, where a focus on health issues has helped the local BME population access drug treatment services, and provided a specialist diabetes nurse to help local GPs offer a targeted service.

Or take Rhondda Housing Association in South Wales, which in addition to its core business of housing provides a range of other opportunities for local people of all ages – from after-school clubs, to youth training, to parental support classes, to environmental action. Indeed, many of the stories here show how social housing landlords are going beyond the bricks and mortar to make their estates safer, cleaner, greener places to live.

This guide gives a range of excellent examples of just what sound neighbourhood management can deliver for residents and communities. I hope it will inspire many more organisations and individuals to get involved.

Rt Hon Ruth Kelly MP
Secretary of State for Communities and Local Government and Minister for Women

About the authors

Pete Duncan and Sally Thomas are co-directors of Social Regeneration Consultants. SRC is based in north east England. It specialises in community-based urban regeneration, working closely with local communities, local authorities and other regeneration agencies on a broad range of initiatives.

The authors have considerable hands-on experience of neighbourhood-based programmes and particularly neighbourhood management. They have worked for local authorities, housing associations and co-operatives, government agencies, community groups and voluntary sector organisations, as employees, board members, advisers, authors and external evaluators. They wrote the CIH publication *Neighbourhood Management: A Good Practice Guide*, published in 2001.

Acknowledgements

The research, writing and publication of this guide were supported by the Housing Corporation, Communities and Local Government, and the Chartered Institute of Housing; the views in it do not necessarily represent those of these organisations.

Adrian Moran of the Housing Corporation and Richard Crossley of CLG have given invaluable support and advice throughout the project.

The following people gave their time to read and comment on the text at various stages; their feedback was much appreciated:

Jas Bains	Ashram Housing Association
Nigel Minto	Association of London Government
Bill Randall	Councillor, Brighton & Hove Council
Peter Richmond	Castle Vale Community Housing Association
Sarah Davis	Chartered Institute of Housing
John Perry	Chartered Institute of Housing
Marie Vernon	Chartered Institute of Housing
Martin Winn	Chartered Institute of Housing
John Connell	Communities and Local Government
Anton Draper	Communities and Local Government
Angus Kennedy	Community Regeneration Partnership
Heather Petch	Hact
Kurshida Mirza	Housing Corporation
Nick Mannion	Knutton Cross Heath Neighbourhood Management Pathfinder
Sandra Brown	Local Government Association
Pam Millington	London & Quadrant Housing Association
Gwyneth Taylor	National Federation of ALMOs
Gary Smith	Transform North Devon Neighbourhood Management Pathfinder
Howard Farrand	Whitefriars Housing Group
Jan Hickman	Wolverhampton Partnership
Paul Booth	Wolverhampton Partnership

Thanks are also due to the many organisations and individuals who offered their views and experience about successful neighbourhoods and contributed good practice examples from around the UK.

CHAPTER 1

INTRODUCTION

About this guide

Creating and sustaining successful neighbourhoods is a major goal of urban policy. This guide explains how housing providers and others can help turn this key government aspiration into practical reality.

Many neighbourhoods are, of course, already successful; they are places where people enjoy a good quality of life, where local services meet their needs and where serious problems are few and far between. In other neighbourhoods, however, changing aspirations, under-investment in the physical infrastructure, poor quality services, an over-concentration of low income households and familiar problems of anti-social behaviour, crime and lack of opportunity have undermined people's quality of life and pitched some formerly stable neighbourhoods into decline.

Successive governments and local service providers have struggled to find the solution to turning these neighbourhoods round. Despite a strong political commitment to narrowing the gap between deprived neighbourhoods and the rest across a broad range of indicators, the seemingly endless string of regeneration initiatives and significant investment of both public and private funds over the past 30 years or so, many 'unsuccessful' neighbourhoods have stubbornly refused to become 'successful'.

But it doesn't have to be like that. As the case studies featured in this guide show, successful neighbourhoods can be found in some of the most deprived communities in the country, many of them supported by housing providers. Understanding the reasons for their success, spreading the word about them and replicating their experience elsewhere are important aims of this guide.

The guide begins by putting neighbourhoods in a strategic and policy context, focusing in particular on the move towards greater devolution of both services and governance and the implications this has for housing providers. It then looks at the factors that help to create and sustain a successful neighbourhood and how housing providers can help put these factors in place.

Subsequent chapters focus on the neighbourhood agenda in more detail, looking particularly at how to make neighbourhood management work in practice and how local communities can take on a stronger leadership role. The guide concludes with an overview of how housing providers can best respond to the changing neighbourhood agenda and looks ahead to future changes.

What is a neighbourhood?

Neighbourhoods are complex places. They are not easy to define, come in different shapes and sizes and often have fluid boundaries. This is, of course, what makes them so interesting – and challenging – for those attempting to make them successful. Efforts by policy-makers and academics to define their scale have resulted in a wide spread of working figures. The fact that the 35 neighbourhood management pathfinders range between 2,000 and 9,000 households demonstrates that a 'one-size fits all' approach is not appropriate for neighbourhood policy.

Many neighbourhoods define themselves – they have obvious physical boundaries, a predominant tenure or building style, or a distinct social make-up. They can also define themselves by property values, or are recognised locally as 'better off' or 'poorer'. The quality of a neighbourhood's physical environment is important, and not only for existing residents – it attracts or puts off potential new residents and investors. But it is not the only factor in determining success, or where a particular neighbourhood starts and ends.

Local perceptions and 'social glue' – the often unseen ties between people in a community – are frequently much more important than physical characteristics in defining a neighbourhood. In many deprived urban areas, people live out their lives in tightly knit, fairly self-contained mini-neighbourhoods. Often just a few streets in extent, these mini-neighbourhoods are important to people; they are the places where they feel reasonably comfortable, where most people know one another and children can be watched over by their families and friends.

In many places both young and older people often have a particularly strong sense of neighbourhood. Young people may define their own neighbourhood 'territories' and will not cross a road, knowing that it could provoke unwanted confrontation. Fear of crime can change people's perception of neighbourhood boundaries, particularly among older residents. More successful neighbourhoods tend to be places where people are not constrained by physical, social or perceptual boundaries, reaching out to other places through a complex series of interactions.

All this means it is not easy to generalise about what a neighbourhood actually is – they are all different, they are never static and people's perceptions about them vary, and change over time. It can be a tricky job to define neighbourhood boundaries which residents, local stakeholders and policy-makers can all sign up to. The temptation to follow political boundaries with their accompanying statistical indicators is often hard to resist, but these rarely coincide with community perceptions about where their neighbourhood starts and ends. Many residents are unaware that they live in an externally defined neighbourhood until the local authority or another agency announces a regeneration initiative. Working with local communities to define neighbourhoods is likely to be an important factor in achieving successful outcomes.

Managing neighbourhoods

Every neighbourhood needs managing, but some need a much lighter touch than others. For many communities, getting involved in the often complex arrangements for managing and delivering neighbourhood services is unnecessary – most people want their bins emptied regularly, their streets cleaned properly and the police to arrive promptly when called. Provided the basics happen, many neighbourhoods work reasonably successfully without being actively managed.

However, in most deprived urban and some rural neighbourhoods, a complex web of interrelated problems means that the 'light touch' approach is not enough and some form of active management is appropriate. The management of neighbourhoods takes many forms, but one particular model has emerged over the past five years, championed by Communities and Local Government – neighbourhood management.

Neighbourhood management was a major element in the 2001 National Strategy for Neighbourhood Renewal, a key component of the government's agenda to narrow the gap between the most deprived parts of the country and the rest. Although often challenging to put in place, it has proved to be very popular and successful – there are already over 250 initiatives across the country, and both national and local evaluations suggest that it has a beneficial impact on people's quality of life.

Examined in more detail in chapter 5, neighbourhood management is a long-term process and is certainly not a quick fix for unsuccessful neighbourhoods. So far, it has been about:

- Re-shaping and localising public services, tailoring them more precisely to local circumstances and needs
- Increasing the takeup of these services by communities
- Improving co-ordination between public services – eg collecting the rubbish *before* cleaning the streets
- Re-allocating resources within and between service providers – to make sure neighbourhood priorities are tackled

- Changing corporate policies – moving from the central to the local
- Changing corporate culture – emphasising the customer, not the provider
- Devolving responsibility for decision-making about detailed service delivery issues down to neighbourhood level and giving local people a say in these decisions, their implementation and outcomes.

The approach taken by the various initiatives across the country has varied significantly, as has their ability to tackle the demanding agenda set out above. Most neighbourhood management initiatives involve, as a minimum, a neighbourhood manager with a small supporting team, community outreach and development workers, neighbourhood wardens and some mechanism for community engagement. Some of the more successful initiatives are much larger, with seconded service providers working in neighbourhood teams based in neighbourhood offices and reporting to elected neighbourhood boards.

Far from being a static model, neighbourhood management is evolving in response to lessons learned from the early initiatives and to the shaping of policy. For example, the concept of community leadership is now moving to centre stage: the government's four year review of the National Strategy for Neighbourhood Renewal, published in 2005, made it clear that neighbourhood management is not only about improving local services, but also about ensuring they are *'led by customers rather than providers'*.

So the way we manage neighbourhoods is already beginning to change; the basic model has worked well and certainly needs to be more widely available, but it also needs an upgrade. It needs to fit with the emerging policy agenda for neighbourhoods – a mix of more extensive decentralisation, community asset ownership and a new emphasis on neighbourhood governance and greater local accountability. This is a policy area where the pace of change is very rapid. Key documents developing the agenda have appeared throughout the period of researching this guide, and no doubt there are plenty more to come. The aim of this guide is to ensure that housing providers, at least, are equipped with the tools they need to respond positively and innovatively to the new agenda.

Who is the guide for?

This guide is aimed mainly at housing professionals and other people who are directly involved in managing and renewing neighbourhoods. It should also be of interest to a broad range of policy-makers, community stakeholders and people active in their own communities.

The research for the guide was mainly confined to England, where the neighbourhood agenda is a top government priority for tackling social exclusion. The authors are, however, aware of parallel initiatives in both Scotland and Wales. Creating and sustaining successful neighbourhoods is a key priority for both the National Assembly for Wales and the Scottish Parliament and there is certainly scope for sharing good practice across national boundaries.

Housing organisations are often the largest stakeholders in deprived urban neighbourhoods and they play an important role in many rural neighbourhoods as well. They have a direct interest in creating and sustaining successful neighbourhoods and many of them play an active role in supporting and, in some cases, leading, neighbourhood management initiatives. Over the past few years they have built up their skills, knowledge and capacity in this area. Much of the good practice guidance set out here has been drawn from their experience up and down the country.

As the role of housing providers in improving neighbourhoods begins to change, many of them will want to be at the forefront of the delivery process – building on their existing expertise and adapting it to the neighbourhood agenda. This guide should help them do so.

CHAPTER 2

NEIGHBOURHOODS: THE POLICY CONTEXT

This chapter puts neighbourhoods in their current broad policy context and explains how a raft of government initiatives, including devolution and local government modernisation, are intended to fit together to deliver neighbourhood change and tackle social exclusion. The chapter ends by looking at the implications of the neighbourhood agenda for housing providers.

As the government's modernisation agenda continues, the relationships between many of the key players are beginning to change. The early emphasis on tackling social exclusion and narrowing the gap between the poorest neighbourhoods and the rest, through targeted urban renewal and better management of local services, has now been supplemented by a re-thinking of the roles and responsibilities of central government, local authorities, social housing providers, local stakeholders and communities. Neighbourhoods are part of a hierarchy of geographical and political places and spaces which has a high degree of inter-dependency. Exploring these inter-relationships – putting neighbourhoods in context – is important.

Devolution – a changing landscape

Devolution, once focused almost exclusively on the governance of Scotland, Wales and Northern Ireland, has now been broadened and deepened to encompass the whole relationship between government and the governed at every level. Cascading power and responsibility from national to regional, sub-regional or local authorities, and from local authorities to neighbourhoods and their communities is now an important part of the modernisation agenda.

This move to devolve power and decentralise is not new, but it is now beginning to permeate every aspect of policy. It is a central plank of the efforts to join up government more effectively. The concept, if not the practice, is also broadly supported by all the major political parties in the UK. Devolution, it would seem, is here to stay.

None of this is without its tensions and contradictions, of course. While police forces have been encouraged to grow larger through amalgamation, neighbourhood policing has become a priority; the move towards elected regional government has been effectively derailed by one adverse referendum; despite their new role as scrutineers and now champions of community calls for action, local councillors have lost some of their political influence as local authorities are run by cabinets, executives and, in some cases, elected mayors (see chapter 5 for more on this). In the housing field, local authorities have become important strategic enablers, and many have transferred their housing stock to maximise investment, while the biggest housing associations have grown steadily larger, as well as much more geographically and functionally diverse, through transfers and amalgamations.

The government's modernisation agenda

The emphasis on devolution – decentralising power from the centre to the local – is increasingly seen by government as the best way of making sure services meet the needs and aspirations of communities. 'Joining things up', empowering individual citizens and communities, giving them a real stake in their neighbourhoods and making service providers much more accountable to them should all be very much part of the agenda. In appropriate areas of policy, central government's task in the new agenda is to loosen its control, transferring power, responsibility and budgets to local authority level, while setting strategic frameworks.

This new agenda is essentially about changing the basis of the relationship between central government, local government and neighbourhoods. It has three main components:

- Reshaping Whitehall, so it is much less involved in the minutiae of what happens in our hospitals, schools and local authorities and much more focused on areas where it has a valuable 'hands-on' role to play

- Reshaping local authorities, so they are better able to govern, strengthen their democratic accountability and are able to control spending

- Encouraging the growth of more neighbourhood bodies, some with new powers, especially over local services, with opportunities for local communities to have a much greater influence over what happens in their neighbourhoods.

***Strong and Prosperous Communities:* The Local Government White Paper (2006)** envisages:

- An increasing emphasis on neighbourhoods
- Further joining up of service planning and delivery, both in neighbourhoods and across and between local authority areas
- A move towards more unitary local authorities
- A stronger strategic leadership role for local authorities
- An enhanced role for local councillors as community advocates
- More opportunities for social housing tenants to develop tenant management
- Greater empowerment of local people
- A performance management approach based on more local targets.

The White Paper puts forward a number of mechanisms for achieving these changes, including:

- The possible restructuring of two-tier local authorities
- Neighbourhood charters
- A further expansion of neighbourhood management and encouragement of tenant management organisations
- A recognition of the need to co-ordinate community capacity building
- Encouraging the transfer of neighbourhood assets to local communities
- Devolved management and contract arrangements and longer funding settlements
- The use of new mechanisms to ensure that action is taken by service providers to redress problems, including a community call for action
- The extension of powers to establish parish councils.

An Implementation Plan for the White Paper, which followed in early 2007, envisaged community calls for action and new parish council arrangements being up and running from 2008. The Local Government and Public Involvement in Health Bill sets the framework to deliver these changes.

The Local Government White Paper's themes can be seen in a number of other documents which point to a significant shift in the power relationship between those responsible for delivery and those in receipt of the outcomes:

***Building Communities, Beating Crime* Home Office White Paper (2004)** and the **Police and Justice Act 2006**

- Neighbourhood policing
- Community call for action if local people feel a community safety issue has not been tackled.

***Our Health, Our Care, Our Say* White Paper (2006)** and the **Local Government and Public Involvement in Health Bill**

- A stronger voice for local communities in the commissioning and provision of health and social care services
- Community call for action.

Education White Paper (2005)

- Shift towards 'trust schools' with greater autonomy
- Shift in the role of the local education authority, from direct provider to strategic commissioning and driving up standards
- More rights, more choice and better support for parents.

Previous key documents in the housing and regeneration fields, the **Sustainable Communities Plan (2003)** and the **Barker Review of Housing Supply (2004)** emphasised partnership and joined-up delivery in order to achieve sustainable neighbourhoods and communities.

Narrowing the gap – tackling social exclusion

Neighbourhoods themselves had already featured as the centrepiece of the National Strategy for Neighbourhood Renewal (2001), the result of a detailed three-year analysis of how to stop decline in the country's poorest neighbourhoods. Under the National Strategy Action Plan, all the poorest neighbourhoods were given common goals of lower worklessness and crime, better health, skills, housing and physical environment. The real challenge was to narrow the gap, on these measures, between the most deprived neighbourhoods and the rest of the country. Neighbourhood renewal and neighbourhood management were seen as two of the main delivery mechanisms. Empowering communities was, and still is, an important theme running through all the policy guidance.

A Neighbourhood Renewal Unit was established in the Office of the Deputy Prime Minister (now the Communities and Local Government department), to spearhead these and other important initiatives. It supported Neighbourhood Renewal teams in each government office for the regions.

The impact of the National Strategy Action Plan on narrowing the gap has yet to be fully tested. Mid-term evaluation work on the New Deal for Communities programme suggested that these high-profile initiatives were beginning to narrow the gap in their neighbourhoods, but only against some measures – predominantly in reducing worklessness, improving educational attainment, and reducing crime but not yet in health, housing and the physical environment.

Parallel evaluation work on the neighbourhood management pathfinders has found that policing and environmental services have improved significantly, with housing, health and schools all making important contributions. However, other service providers have been less willing to embrace the neighbourhood agenda. But it is still early days and, as yet, evidence on whether neighbourhood management itself is helping to narrow the gap is still patchy. This issue is dealt with in more detail in chapter 5 of the guide. Before that, chapter 4 explores efforts to strengthen the many neighbourhoods whose relative deprivation has remained unchanged for decades.

Regional devolution

There has always been a measure of government devolution to the English regions, with regional development agencies (RDAs), regional assemblies and the single pot being recent manifestations. First set up in 1999, RDAs have focused primarily on economic and sustainable development. Government offices for the regions currently represent ten government departments at regional level.

Government support for regions has traditionally been channelled through these regional agencies and direct to local authorities and in some cases, deprived neighbourhoods. In recent years, however, there has been a recognition that neighbourhoods and local authorities are too small, and regions too big, to deliver greater urban competitiveness. But there has also been a growing recognition that tackling social exclusion and narrowing the deprivation gap depends, to a great extent, on lifting the economic performance of both individual cities and groups of cities within a region.

Consequently, cities have been encouraged to join together within regions, to raise their profile, pool resources, strengthen their joint economies and become more competitive. This agenda, currently still under discussion, offers the prospect of further devolution of central government power and responsibilities. Each city-region could potentially have the freedom, flexibility and funding to pursue its own priorities, albeit within an agreed strategic framework. The Northern Way represents the first attempts to join up city regions to achieve macro-regional economic change.

The changing role of local government

One step down the devolution ladder, the role of local government has changed significantly over the past twenty years and continues to do so. Following the interim report from the Lyons Inquiry into the role and functions of local government, the Local

Government White Paper (2006) presages another significant change to the way local authorities conduct their business, holding out the prospect of greater autonomy and a strengthened local democracy. A second report by Sir Michael Lyons, published in March 2007, focuses on how local authorities are financed. It has endorsed this broad approach, proposing greater flexibility, transparency and incentives for local government in the future.

Twenty years ago, most local authorities were major providers of local services, significant asset holders and strategic policy-makers and deliverers. Now, they have essentially two core functions: an increasingly strategic and commissioning role in service delivery, often in partnership with other providers, and the role of 'place-making' in urban and rural areas alike. Local authorities now have more powers at their disposal than they have ever had, and need the commitment and creativity to put them to good use.

The Local Government Act 2000 in particular gave them wide-ranging powers to improve the economic, social or environmental wellbeing of their area and the requirement to produce Sustainable Community Strategies. But most feel constrained, not liberated, by their new, slimmed-down role. They need to build up their capacity to make best use of their powers, while the introduction of public-private partnerships, particularly in the regeneration field, demands stronger partnership skills and the benefit of further experience.

Some local authorities are still adapting to their strategic role. Where an authority no longer owns stock it sometimes means that they also have less housing expertise and clout to lever in other funding to support their strategic aims. Those that do have housing stock, however, often continue to concentrate their strategic activities around it, limiting their vision and resulting in a narrow focus on social housing.

Changes in the role of local government have been accompanied by a significant reduction in some of its resources. The ability of local authorities to mount significant capital programmes has been constrained by the need to dispose of assets. This has reduced their influence over the way many local services are provided, creating new partnerships, but also new tensions along the way. It has not been an easy learning curve.

Following the joint CIH-LGA report *Visionary Leadership in Housing: a new future for local housing strategy*, CIH is continuing to work with the LGA, the Housing Corporation, the IDeA (Improvement and Development Agency) and others to provide information and learning opportunities geared to equipping professionals with the skills to undertake this important strategic function.

Local Area Agreements

One of the bright spots for local government in recent years has been the government's piloting of Local Area Agreements (LAAs) – three year partnership programmes that aim to pool and simplify funding streams, join up local services more effectively and reduce Whitehall intervention in four fields: children and young people, safer and stronger communities, healthier communities and older people, and economic development and enterprise.

Introduced to extend the Local Public Service Agreements, strengthen the National Strategy for Neighbourhood Renewal and begin the process of rationalising the plethora of area-based initiatives, LAAs are a key component of the devolution agenda. A strengthened role for government offices, with reduced Whitehall supervision, indicates an important change of emphasis.

Although their impact is not yet fully apparent, Local Area Agreements certainly have the potential to make a significant contribution to the new agenda for neighbourhoods. The success of LAAs will depend, in part, on how local authorities and their partners respond to their new joined-up role, building on the experience of their local strategic partnerships, and also on how quickly central government itself adapts to the hands-off, single pot philosophy for public spending on local services, including the Neighbourhood Renewal Fund.

New roles for service providers

The increasing emphasis on partnership working and joining up has focused in particular on the role and activities of **Local Strategic Partnerships (LSPs)**. They have brought together a range of key public, private and voluntary sector partners to draw up and deliver, through their partners, community strategies and neighbourhood renewal, broadening some decision-making beyond local authorities and helping to join up service delivery

Recent evaluation work suggests that there remains some blurring of responsibilities between LSPs and local authorities, acknowledges problems with constraining some LSPs within local authority boundaries and recommends reviewing partners, to ensure that the right organisations are involved and that they are represented at the right level. There has also been a lack of significant engagement by the private sector and some questioning of the capacity of the community sector to engage fully in the LSP process.

At local authority level, there has been a proliferation of other new governance structures, many involving partnerships between service providers and local communities. This broadening out of decision-making responsibility is not without its complications. In cities the size of Bradford, local authority estimates suggest that more than 3,500 local volunteers are needed to fill all the governance positions in these and many other relatively new organisations.

Not surprisingly, some places have been difficult to fill and there are some concerns that 'initiative fatigue' may now be entrenched. Nevertheless, volunteering is increasing nationally, with more than one million people actively supporting their communities in various ways. Despite the many problems, partnership working is undoubtedly here to stay.

There remain many policy contradictions and there are doubts that government can square the circle in its drives for greater efficiency and double devolution. As Marilyn Taylor's recent work for the Joseph Rowntree Foundation has shown, there remains an implementation gap, with different policy priorities often pulling in opposite directions. Nowhere are these tensions more obvious than in the social housing sector.

From decent homes to mixed, sustainable communities: the implications for housing providers

Housing providers are, or certainly should be, at the centre of this broad policy agenda. They are important strategic players in most local authorities and in many neighbourhoods; they own and control significant assets that give them considerable financial and political leverage; they have experience and expertise in working with communities that many other service providers do not have. The 2007 Hills Review (CLG) into the future of social housing takes a wide view of the sector's potential. In particular, there is a focus on how existing and new social housing can contribute to places that are well designed and attractive, how providers can work towards developing mixed communities rather than the monolithic estates of the past, and how access to a wider range of housing options can be developed according to changes in income and aspiration. Perhaps most importantly, however, in the wider context of successful neighbourhoods, there is a clear steer on the need to view good social housing as but one element of a successful neighbourhood, partnered by measures to address, in particular, worklessness and economic disadvantage. Hills sees housing providers as not simply investing in their stock but also in the other aspects of neighbourhoods for which they are responsible.

It may therefore come as a surprise to many outside observers that housing in general, and housing associations in particular, are not always centre stage in neighbourhood matters. The Gershon drive towards efficiency, which has led to reducing the number of Primary Care Trusts through amalgamations, and to proposals for mergers of police forces as well as a raft of area-based regeneration initiatives, has also impacted on the housing sector. The forthcoming organisation of the Housing Corporation, English Partnerships and part of CLG to create Communities England, and the seemingly relentless mergers between housing associations to create ever larger and more financially powerful groupings is changing the face of social housing. Many housing associations in England are now big business; but they are not yet punching their weight in the neighbourhood arena.

During the past ten years or so, many housing associations have focused on the key objectives of expansion and rationalisation, and attracting private finance into new-build development projects. Over the same period, most local authority housing providers have been focused on the different, but not unrelated agenda of stock transfers and the creation of ALMOs, and bringing their housing stock up to the Decent Homes Standard by 2010. Much has changed in all these areas:

- One million local authority homes have been transferred to new or existing housing associations
- 64 ALMOs have been created to take on the management of about one million local authority homes
- Housing associations now manage more than two million homes; the largest housing association groups now own and manage more than 50,000 homes
- The number of registered social landlords has fallen, due to mergers and deregulation, but still stands at 1,500
- £30 billion of private finance has been injected into social housing provision, with a further £10 billion anticipated by 2010
- 3.6 million homes provided by social landlords will be at or close to the Decent Homes Standard by 2010.

Many housing associations have also been closely involved in regeneration initiatives, taking the lead on major projects in some cases. Their involvement has often been crucial to successful delivery and many are now working in close partnership with private housebuilders and local authorities. Some of these providers have also taken a lead role in the wider neighbourhood agenda.

Despite these significant achievements, the focus on corporate growth and finance has inevitably meant that most housing associations have not given enough attention to the strategic devolution issue as it has risen up the policy agenda. Many of them are still grappling with delivering decent homes while the agenda has shifted to creating and sustaining mixed communities and neighbourhoods. Most are still seen by government as one-dimensional organisations rather than the multi-dimensional bodies some already are and others aspire to be. This has had a direct impact on how they are perceived and their role in the developing neighbourhood and strategic devolution agenda. For example:

- The initial wave of Local Area Agreements omitted the physical and built environment, including housing provision, although there are indications that this may be remedied in future rounds

- Housing providers did not have a prominent role in the first round of neighbourhood management pathfinders, something that was remedied in the second round

- None of the fourteen community cohesion pathfinders had more than a limited housing focus

- Perhaps more surprisingly, few housing associations are yet represented on Local Strategic Partnerships' main bodies, although they are often found on the subcommittees

- Housing associations have generally been slow to exploit neighbourhood funding regimes, such as the Neighbourhood Renewal Fund and the Safer and Stronger Communities Fund

- Although there are more than 200 tenant management organisations in local authority housing stock, there are very few examples of housing associations devolving management responsibility to their tenants – those that do exist are usually the result of pre-existing devolution arrangements being continued following stock transfer.

Despite the National Housing Federation's timely iN business initiative, which exhorts housing associations to play a more proactive role in neighbourhoods, there remain doubts about the collective determination to put it into practice. There is a feeling in some circles that housing providers are inclined to follow rather than lead agendas for change in this area; that, with some notable exceptions, the publicity has outstripped delivery when it comes to neighbourhoods and communities.

Although many housing providers may regard this as an unfair analysis, there is no doubt that these external perceptions are real and changing them is a continuing challenge. If housing providers are to play a key role in delivering the neighbourhood agenda – as they must – they need to start with a significant re-ordering of their corporate priorities.

Housing providers are part of an emerging political and professional consensus about the need to increase the importance of neighbourhoods; to give them a status they have not had before and increase the involvement and influence of the people who live and work there. A new neighbourhood agenda is emerging. The next chapter outlines how this may be rolled out over the next few years.

CHAPTER 3

THE NEIGHBOURHOOD AGENDA

This chapter focuses on the neighbourhood agenda, some of it outlined in the 2006 Local Government White Paper, including community calls for action, local charters, new governance arrangements and community asset ownership. It concludes with advice on what housing providers can do to help deliver this potentially challenging agenda.

The neighbourhood agenda is essentially about two key ambitions: improving public services and re-engaging people with government. Focusing on neighbourhoods involves a number of new activities and further development of those that are already being tested – such as neighbourhood management. The broad aims are to:

- Make a real difference to the quality of local services and how well they respond to community views and aspirations in neighbourhoods
- Increase the involvement of communities in making decisions about these local services and about the life of their neighbourhood
- Give opportunities for public service providers and voluntary and community groups to work together to deliver real change for the neighbourhood
- Build the capacity of communities to engage fully in neighbourhood change, by strengthening social capital, reducing isolation and promoting community cohesion.

So what is this likely to mean in practice? This part of the guide looks at three interrelated themes :

- Devolving power and responsibility to neighbourhoods
- Strengthening neighbourhood governance
- Encouraging community ownership of local assets.

There is detailed good practice advice about strengthening links between service providers and communities in chapter 5 and about building community capacity in chapter 6.

Devolving power and responsibility to the neighbourhood

Community concerns are often very local – most people 'think local' – so any initiative that gives them more influence and control over their neighbourhoods is likely to be widely welcomed. However, it must deliver a real difference to people's lives. The responsibilities taken on by neighbourhoods need to be tailored to local circumstances, be flexible enough to allow change and be responsive to the wider community and organisations active locally. There is also a need for appropriate arrangements, including sustained capacity-building, for engaging communities fully in the decision-making process.

Neighbourhood service delivery

The neighbourhood agenda will only succeed if service providers are willing to engage in it. Service providers need to see neighbourhoods not only as a focus for their activities, but also as places where they negotiate agreements on how those services are to be delivered.

Neighbourhood bodies will need to decide how they want service providers to be involved and strike the appropriate agreements with them about delivery. There will inevitably be time and cost efficiency issues to consider. Integration between services needs to be both horizontal and vertical if neighbourhood delivery is to be fully coordinated.

These arrangements will vary significantly between neighbourhoods, but may include:

- Setting neighbourhood priorities for a range of services
- Direct and regular consultation with service providers
- Devolved decisions about the nature and scope of individual services
- Direct responsibility by neighbourhood bodies for some budgets
- Management by neighbourhood bodies of service delivery in some cases
- Arrangements for redress if service delivery does not meet agreed standards.

Neighbourhood services, neighbourhood control

INCLUDE NEIGHBOURHOOD REGENERATION, LIVERPOOL

Delivering local services is a central theme of Include, a neighbourhood regeneration company based in the Dingle area of Liverpool 8. Through community consultation, local people said their main priority was a *'clean, safe and well managed neighbourhood'*.

→

Clean

Include Environmental Services was launched in 2002. It is a community-based social enterprise employing local people to deliver a range of services including:

- Improving 'grot spots'
- Grounds maintenance and grass cutting
- Tackling fly-tipping
- Graffiti removal.

As well as maintaining the residential areas, the business has expanded its operations, providing services to a range of commercial clients across Merseyside.

Safe

Include's Safer Neighbourhoods Project focuses on crime and community safety, adopting a partnership approach with the neighbourhood police and Liverpool ASB Unit through a range of projects which include alley gating, CCTV, ASBOs and ABAs and quad bike patrols in local parks.

Well managed

The management of the area is coordinated from the locally-based Include Centre for Neighbourhood Management. The centre brings together 75 staff from a wide range of agencies, including the city council.

Holding neighbourhood service providers to account

If there is one universal weakness in most neighbourhood-based programmes it is the failure to establish a credible link between agreement about what needs to be done and subsequent action on the ground. Many communities, although not always suffering from consultation fatigue, have become cynical about the motives of major agencies, particularly local authorities, largely because of this gap between intention and action. Liverpool City Council uses a phrase that deserves wider adoption: *'No excuses, just do it!'*

When public services fail to meet local expectations, and particularly where they do not meet agreed standards of delivery, communities need to know why and be able to initiate positive action. There need to be mechanisms which enable people, through established neighbourhood organisations and their locally elected councillors, to hold service providers to account and get things done within a reasonable timescale.

Such mechanisms should form part of neighbourhood management agreements, contracts or charters (the terminology is not important), which set out what service providers agree to do and specify the redress available to neighbourhood communities if they don't deliver. In some circumstances, these arrangements could be extended to local communities agreeing to do one thing in return for a service provider doing another – for example, community management of an open space or playground, in return for investment in new play equipment.

The concept of neighbourhood redress could be particularly useful when dealing with anti-social behaviour. Under new regulations a local authority can, if it chooses and the TMO is willing, delegate responsibilities for ASBOs to a TMO (tenant management organisation).

Communities could also benefit from having some say over how service provider budgets are spent in their neighbourhoods. Some budgets (though not all) could certainly be devolved from the centre, to neighbourhood boards, as a way of increasing community control.

The 2006 Local Government White Paper and the Local Government and Public Involvement in Health Bill proposals make a start on delivering this important part of the neighbourhood agenda, in particular by:

- Introducing the concept of **community calls for action**, enabling local councillors to hold service providers to account, following representations from local communities
- Proposing a wider use of **neighbourhood charters** – voluntary agreements between local communities, local authorities and other service providers – setting out standards, targets and priorities and providing opportunities for neighbourhoods to take responsibility for some functions and facilities themselves.

Strengthening neighbourhood governance

There are currently many types of governance arrangements that impact on neighbourhoods, and this section looks at a range of them.

Parish and town councils

There are around 10,000 parish and town councils in England and Wales, with the smallest covering just 200 people and the largest as many as 70,000. The Quality Parish Scheme, set up in 2003, was an attempt to boost the role of the best of them, taking on services and facilities normally controlled at district or county level. Their powers were further extended in 2005 and 2006, enabling them to take responsibility for keeping their neighbourhoods clean, provide attractive public spaces and tackle anti-social behaviour. In some cases, this has had a significant beneficial impact on local people, giving them more direct control; in others, local authorities have been reluctant to devolve further powers to parish councils, something they are now being encouraged to do more widely.

The Local Government White Paper (2006) envisages a further expansion of parish councils across England, with more being established in urban areas and providing new opportunities for their creation in London. However, it recognises, rightly, that other forms of neighbourhood governance may be more appropriate in many cases and cautions against parish councils where community cohesion may be compromised.

Area committees

Area committees have a formal role within a local authority's decision-making system. They enable local councillors to take decisions on delegated matters at a more local level, often with small budgets, but only a small proportion deal with issues outside the remit of the local authority. This and their often large geographical scope mean they are not neighbourhood bodies. They are rarely well-attended by the public and have a limited role to play in neighbourhood governance.

The role of local councillors

The Local Government Act (2000) introduced a slimmer, more focused decision-making framework for elected councillors, based around executive cabinets and, in some cases, elected mayors. This may have improved the efficiency of decision-making, but it has also coincided with lower voter participation in local elections and increasing public distrust and general dissatisfaction with the democratic system. There is a widely acknowledged 'democratic deficit' and the future role of local councillors has been uncertain – something the Local Government White Paper (2006) aims to address.

Local councillors certainly need a clear and coherent role. Some are becoming neighbourhood advocates, with a much wider brief than simply representing the local authority at neighbourhood level. They are beginning to combine their representational role with one that helps to empower local communities. As well as their strategic role within the council's area, their role as community advocate now includes:

- Speaking up for and on behalf of neighbourhood individuals and groups
- Encouraging communities to engage in neighbourhood issues
- Participating in the planning process
- Communicating community issues to the local authority and other service providers.

Local councillors' role as community leaders also involves:

- Giving local communities a voice and encouraging individuals and groups to use it – principally now through community calls for action
- Helping communities become self-propelled
- Acting as a useful link between service providers and users at neighbourhood level
- Acting as a broker between a range of interests and partners.

These new roles are reflected in the Local Government White Paper (2006), which sees local councillors as local 'democratic champions'. Many local councillors would agree that they need support, training and perhaps even 'cultural re-alignment' if they are to deliver this new role effectively. There is more on the changing role of local councillors in chapter 5.

Area forums and neighbourhood management boards

Area forums usually act as sounding boards on neighbourhood issues, while neighbourhood management boards often have specific responsibilities for coordinating service delivery and managing specific neighbourhood-based programmes. They operate within defined neighbourhoods, often crossing ward boundaries, with average populations of 4-5,000 households. There is more on neighbourhood management boards in chapter 5.

These types of semi-formal structures are now very popular – more than half of all local authorities have area forums and as many as 4 in every 5 have partnership organisations of one form or another. Neighbourhood management boards are still relatively few and far between, but are increasing significantly as more local authorities shift the focus of service delivery and partnership working to neighbourhood level and begin to engage more closely with local communities.

Community-based housing organisations

Community-based and controlled housing organisations come in many different forms and there are now more than 500 of them in England. Community-based housing associations, housing co-ops and tenant management organisations provide mainly social housing for local communities. Most of those that own housing stock are registered with the Housing Corporation as social landlords, while others are unregistered, working in partnership with local authorities and registered social landlords. A relatively new model, known as Community Gateway, is being piloted in several areas as a way of providing community and tenant control over large-scale voluntary transfers. CIH has published a separate guide on this subject *Empowering Communities – the Community Gateway* model (see page 106).

The common theme across all of these housing bodies is their control by local communities, although in England most are tenant-based organisations. Many of them operate as umbrellas for an increasingly broad range of neighbourhood activities, moving well beyond their traditional role as housing providers or managers. Independent evaluation work on tenant management organisations has found that they are often better housing managers than other housing providers, matching the performance of the top 25% of local authorities in England.

Community trusts

Development Trusts are not-for-profit enterprises, usually community-led and generating income through a range of activities, often focused on local economic development and asset ownership. They vary considerably in size and the existing network of several hundred trusts now appears to be expanding rapidly. Most have a very 'can-do' culture.

Community Land Trusts are a relatively new type of community-controlled organisation that own, develop or manage local assets (buildings, land and houses) for community benefit. Often operating in a small rural or suburban neighbourhood, they use local physical assets to create wealth and retain it in the local economy. See chapter 6 for more details.

Neighbourhood forums and community councils

Neighbourhood forums or community councils are committees of volunteers and are usually sponsored by local authorities. Most are run as sounding boards, with no delegated decision-making powers, but increasingly they are providing important platforms for local communities concerned about the future of their neighbourhoods. Their boundaries usually reflect local communities and do not always follow ward boundaries. In most cases, all residents are entitled to be members.

There are many hundreds of these bodies across England. Their common features include the following:

- They are consultative, providing a channel of communication between residents, the council and other organisations
- They are non-political and represent all residents in a specific area, irrespective of tenure
- They hold open public meetings at least once a quarter and decide their own agendas
- They discuss all local and borough-wide issues, not just those involving the local authority

- They are consulted on planning matters and often campaign on specific issues affecting their neighbourhood or community
- They offer a regular opportunity to meet ward councillors and council officers, providing an important link between community activists and agencies.

Community, tenants' and residents' associations

There are many thousands of associations of residents across England. Many are also part of local federations. They are run by local people and are often involved in a multitude of activities, from single issue campaigns against mobile phone masts, to running playgroups and managing spaces in their neighbourhoods. Some have their own community assets. At their best, they are a vital first step on the governance 'ladder'.

Many are informally run with no constitutions, but most operate with a degree of formality and try to be as inclusive and representative as possible. Although they usually have no formal status in local decision-making, they are often consulted by local authorities, housing associations and others about future plans and specific proposals.

The credibility of tenants' and residents' associations with agencies, and particularly local authorities and social housing landlords, usually depends on how representative they are seen to be. There are legitimate concerns about the potential domination of small, but influential neighbourhood organisations by extreme minority voices.

The broader the representation, the more influence these organisations can expect to have. But many find it difficult to be self-propelled – they often need intensive and sustained help from community professionals to help them get there. There is more about community capacity building in chapter 6.

Community asset ownership

All neighbourhoods have community assets – buildings or spaces that are particularly important to local communities – but they are not, by any means, always owned and controlled by local communities. More often than not they are owned by service agencies, with varying degrees of local management. As well as the community-based housing organisations mentioned earlier, community assets that do involve a significant degree of community control (although not always ownership) include the following:

- The growing number of **village** or **community halls**, which are typically quite small, run by volunteers and are financially self-sufficient. There are now nearly 9,000 of these in England, most of them in rural areas.

- Larger **community centres**, mainly in urban areas, usually have more explicit community development aims. They are often run by community associations, working in partnership with local authorities which have tended to retain ownership in the majority of cases. There are more than 4,000 of these centres in England.

- **Multi-purpose centres**, providing a base for a range of services, with paid staff and usually incorporating a community component. There are up to 100 of these centres across England, but only a handful are directly owned and controlled by local communities.

- **Community parks, gardens and allotments** also take many forms, enabling communities to control important and often scarce open space within their neighbourhoods.

In most cases, these have been successful initiatives – many of them have stood the test of time, proving more robust than outside agencies perhaps expected. Others have proved less sustainable. There is more about community asset ownership in chapter 6.

Community-owned assets

WESTWAY DEVELOPMENT TRUST, LONDON

Westway is one of the oldest and most successful development trusts. It was created in response to the building of an elevated motorway through North Kensington which was bringing blight, noise and disruption to an area already contending with deprivation. A four-year campaign by an angry community led to a partnership between community organisations and the borough council. 23 acres of derelict land have been reclaimed and commercial developments, largely focused on the fashion and creative industries, now contribute to the local economy and fund the Trust's charitable activities. Westway also owns a vibrant section of Portobello Market.

Community facilities range from parks to charity workspaces and from fitness facilities to centres for migrant and refugee communities and supplementary schools. The Trust has also created the iconic 8-acre Westway Sports Centre – which includes a youth sports academy and London's leading junior tennis centre. The Trust began with a council grant of £25,000; today it is a self-sufficient charity with a £6 million turnover and assets valued at £30 million. It makes grants to other community organisations and helps set up local projects beyond its immediate boundaries. Over 800 people are now employed on Trust land, where 30 years ago there was just rubble and desolation beneath the flyover.

Gearing up for the new agenda – the implications for housing providers

For housing providers the focus on neighbourhoods presents a crucial opportunity to place themselves, alongside local communities, at the heart of the new agenda. There is already much good work in support of neighbourhoods across the country, but both the government and the Housing Corporation are now keen to see a step-change in the intensity of involvement. Action is needed and expected in the following areas:

- *Adding community value*
- *Encouraging more mixed communities*
- *Joining up with other providers at neighbourhood level*
- *Empowering communities*

Adding community value

Social housing organisations can and should do more than simply provide and manage low-cost housing in neighbourhoods; many already do, viewing it as a social – even a moral – imperative as well as good business. Most already add community value to their housing service through care provision and providing management services for other local organisations. The wider range of initiatives includes:

- Early years provision, including childcare and nurseries
- Employment training and the development of social enterprises
- Local labour initiatives, such as young people's construction schemes
- Community centres and activities for community cohesion and inclusion
- Financial inclusion, including help with setting up credit unions
- Repair and maintenance programmes for private dwellings
- Youth facilities and outreach
- Older people's programmes, including drop-in centres
- Provision of neighbourhood management
- Funding extra local police and community wardens
- One-stop-shop advice centres
- Local environmental initiatives, such as Home Zones and public space projects.

Some housing providers are now also looking at direct financial support for local schools, to maintain successful neighbourhoods and protect their investment.

While the scale of housing association involvement in the broader community value agenda is increasing significantly, there is scope for far greater activity. Registered social landlords are currently allowed to devote up to 49% of their business to non-housing activities, but only 3% of registered social landlords are regarded by the Housing Corporation as officially 'diverse' organisations – where more than 5% of their annual turnover is for non-housing purposes. In 2003/04, 55 associations invested (from various sources) £29 million in adding community value nationally; by 2006 this had increased to £35 million a year in London alone, with £138 million a year in the northern regions expected to be invested over the next five years.

Encouraging more mixed communities

Recent research suggests that most neighbourhoods benefit from diversity and a mix of different people and incomes, and most estates managed by social landlords usually have significant numbers of owner-occupiers who have exercised their right to buy, or bought into the estate, either for their own use or as a buy-to-let investment. In low-income neighbourhoods, the drive to further mix communities is an important one, but there remains a tension between neighbourhood aspirations and meeting housing needs, including those of homeless people, refugees and asylum seekers and other vulnerable groups. The Hills Report into the future of social housing, published in February 2007, highlighted a number of ways in which a better income mix could be achieved on existing social housing estates. These included large-scale remodelling, reviewing allocations and access policies, retaining high income tenants through a raft of neighbourhood initiatives, and more support to improve the incomes and work prospects of existing tenants.

Joining up with other providers

Partnership working between stakeholders, at local and at strategic level, is critical for delivering change in neighbourhoods. Housing providers with significant stock holdings in neighbourhoods have a long-term commitment to an area, and their expertise and support systems put them in a strong position to take the lead in such partnerships.

Housing providers have a good track record of being proactive and innovative, particularly as developers and in providing special needs housing, but less so in terms of ongoing neighbourhood management. There is much to learn from the experiences of those housing associations and ALMOs that are involved with the Round 2 neighbourhood management pathfinders (as well as some that have been running their own initiatives). Chapter 4 provides good practice advice in this area.

Empowering communities

Many housing providers already work closely with their own tenants, through tenants' associations and federations, tenant board members and, in some cases, tenant involvement in managing stock. There are important opportunities for housing providers to help strengthen the wider community to achieve neighbourhood change, and this theme is expanded in chapters 6 and 7. Empowering communities is a long-term community development task – and one not always recognised by regulatory bodies as being of key importance. It is resource intensive, often with uncertain outcomes.

The Elton Review of the regulatory and compliance requirements of registered social landlords called for more emphasis on the neighbourhood as an important level for accountability, resident involvement on every board and committee responsible for service delivery, and resident-led inspection as a way of reducing some of the formal regulatory processes. CIH's subsequent two reports on resident-led self regulation have looked at the potential of this approach and how it could work in practice.

Overall, housing providers should be fully engaged in most, if not all, aspects of the neighbourhood agenda. Picking out a few activities and not rising to the challenge of the rest risks simply replicating the past, rather patchy, response. A more robust, proactive and comprehensive approach to neighbourhoods is now required. These issues are explored in more depth in chapters 5, 6 and 7.

Building community assets

CASTLE VALE COMMUNITY HOUSING ASSOCIATION, BIRMINGHAM

Castle Vale Community Housing Association is run by local people for the benefit of the whole Castle Vale community in north Birmingham. It is one of the few independent housing associations in the country that are managed by boards with a resident majority. It has 2,500 rented homes and community assets of £200 million.

Although housing is by far the biggest community asset in Castle Vale, two important facilities are also under community control:

- The Sanctuary is a multi-purpose community building, offering a range of activities including preventative health initiatives. The association stepped in to stop the charity-run facility from closing.

- The community housing association has also recently bought an old police station that was becoming derelict and was at risk of blighting the community. The financial strength provided by the housing assets enabled them to buy the building before it became a serious problem.

→

Castle Vale provides three important lessons on community asset ownership:

1. Any stock transfer process is likely to be more successful if a genuine community owned vehicle is set up that gives local people real control of the assets. Having local control and the support of the community gives the housing association much more clout and an ability to deliver real change in the neighbourhood.

2. The size of the association and its management experience means that it can deliver real economies of scale to make community assets more viable. It can also tackle the bureaucracy of community asset ownership in a way which smaller bodies often find much more difficult.

3. Having an entirely local focus meant that the association could see the sense in acquiring a derelict, at-risk building and then developing it into a community facility.

Chapter 4

What Makes a Successful Neighbourhood?

This chapter examines the factors that contribute to successful neighbourhoods. Starting with a brief historical perspective, it looks at why some neighbourhoods fail, then focuses on the main ingredients for success, concluding with a section on how successful neighbourhoods can sustain themselves in the future.

Many people already live in successful neighbourhoods; they are places where the majority have a job, where the environment is clean and well-maintained and where crime is minimal. But this is far from being a reality for all.

In the unsuccessful neighbourhoods, anti-social behaviour, crime, poor housing and environment, lack of jobs, inadequate facilities and uncoordinated services combine to limit community expectations, restrict choice and, at the extreme, create a spiral of decline which can lead to abandonment. Despite these problems, many people do have a surprisingly strong attachment to such neighbourhoods. Older people in particular recall friendlier days when neighbours looked out for each other. This nostalgic, rose-tinted view of neighbourhoods has too often been dismissed as an unattainable goal in a modern society.

Times have certainly changed and many of the factors influencing people's satisfaction with their neighbourhoods are now significantly different. Society has become more focused on the individual and less on the collective; the dominance of the car and the arrival of sophisticated computer technology in the majority of homes have both had a significant impact. Nevertheless, the important values and human interaction that underpin neighbourhood nostalgia have not been entirely lost.

Up and down the country, some of the most successful deprived neighbourhoods are those where there is a collective community spirit, where people have organised together, taken control of some aspects of their lives and where they have been fully supported by external agencies. They are by no means the only successful neighbourhoods, but many of them do stand out as beacons of good practice.

The lessons of history

Successful neighbourhoods are not a new phenomenon, but over the past ten years they have been under the spotlight, as governments and policy-makers have grappled with the multiple problems of those that are less successful.

The government's Guide Neighbourhoods programme, launched in 2004 and due to run until 2007, is part of the government's *Together We Can* initiative. Many of the selected neighbourhoods have a long history of community activity and leadership and all are successful in different ways. They are now spreading their message to other places as part of this programme. There is a list of the Guide Neighbourhoods in appendix C.

There has been a tendency to dismiss such neighbourhoods as one-offs that are not replicable elsewhere – the products of interesting, but unique, histories. That is only partially true. In an age when there is a constant demand for innovation it is always worth looking back at what worked in the past and learning the historical lessons. It is not always necessary to re-invent the wheel – sometimes an old one just needs a good dusting down and a new inner tube to make it work.

Two case studies featured here – Bournville Village Trust and the Eldonians have very different histories and are certainly distinct neighbourhoods – the former created by philanthropy and the latter by relentless grass roots campaigning. But they have one thing in common – they are both widely regarded as unique and therefore not really replicable. Failing to learn the lessons from places like Bournville and the Eldonian Village would be a mistake. They have fascinating and highly relevant stories to tell and ones which have important lessons for those involved with creating and sustaining successful neighbourhoods everywhere.

There are other lessons from the past that raise questions about how far it is wise to travel down the devolution road. The connection between what happens in neighbourhoods and what happens at a more strategic level is both important and not easy to get right. In the 1980s and 1990s several local authorities, including Walsall, Tower Hamlets and Islington, introduced radical forms of devolved decision-making which proved not to be sustainable for a variety of reasons.

Simply parcelling up policy and services into neighbourhood-sized chunks is unlikely to deliver what's needed. The connections and synergy between strategic and neighbourhood activity are clearly important, as is the need for organic growth as neighbourhoods find their own way of controlling their destinies.

Learning from the past

BOURNVILLE VILLAGE TRUST, WEST MIDLANDS

Bournville is a popular mixed-tenure neighbourhood in Birmingham that has stood the test of time. It began life at the end of the 19th century as a George Cadbury-sponsored model village. As it grew, several distinct neighbourhoods developed, all with:

- A high quality natural environment
- An imaginative and coherent overall planning framework
- High architectural quality of the built environment
- A socially mixed community
- On-the-spot estate management
- Involvement of the community in the management of the neighbourhoods.

Creating and sustaining a tenure and social mix has always been an important element of the management of the Bournville estate. Experience here suggests that where housing is attractive and well-managed locally, irrespective of tenure, households want to stay longer in their neighbourhood or will commit themselves more to activities within it, ensuring greater social cohesion.

The mix of property types, tenures and house values provides variety, opportunity and choice, and Bournville has managed to avoid becoming a highly polarised community. Bournville could be said to be one of the pioneers of 'tenure-blind' housing.

The Trust has now begun work to create a second Bournville – a new millennium urban village in Telford. It clearly believes Bournville village is replicable elsewhere. It plans to build around 800 new homes with social, leisure and sports facilities, plus commercial and employment opportunities which will make a real community, rather than just another large housing estate.

Community-run neighbourhoods

ELDONIAN VILLAGE, LIVERPOOL

This once deprived post-industrial neighbourhood in Vauxhall, Liverpool, has been turned into a thriving and vibrant community over the last 25 years. The transformation has been led by local residents who were determined to keep their community together and to improve their quality of life.

→

The history of the Eldonians dates back to the 1970s, when the group was set up in response to the city council's plans to clear local tenement blocks. In 1983, following the closure of the Tate and Lyle factory, they formed the Eldonian Housing Co-operative, which led the redevelopment of the site. By 1989, 145 new homes were built on the site and in 1990 the co-op gained housing association status that enabled a further 150 homes to be built.

This development has become known as the Eldonian Village, offering a mixture of family housing and specialist housing for older people, a safe, clean environment, good local facilities and local employment opportunities, all of them owned or managed by the Eldonians themselves.

The community is at the heart of everything. The Eldonian Community Trust, with 600 members, has a social welfare remit and directs activities, the Eldonian Community-Based Housing Association looks after housing management and the Eldonian Group, a development trust, is responsible for the wider economic regeneration of the area and the development of community-based businesses and new developments.

The range of high quality facilities also makes an important contribution to the success of the neighbourhood. Each facility is run as a community-based business providing local employment opportunities. These include:

- A village hall
- Eldonian House, a purpose-built residential care home
- Eldon Woods day nursery
- Elaine Norris Sports Centre
- Catch On! Project – community based therapeutic health care

The Eldonian Village is undoubtedly a successful neighbourhood. It shows what can be achieved through the passion, commitment and vision of local residents.

Why some neighbourhoods fail

It is an uncomfortable fact that 1 in 5 people in the UK still live in income poverty; 17% of children live in households where no-one works; 1 in 5 adults are functionally illiterate. Despite the best efforts of governments and agencies to turn around these depressing statistics, progress has been modest and, on some measures, the position has worsened over the past 20 years. Recent research has suggested that the patterns of economic segregation have changed very little over this period. Although many jobs have been created, they have not usually been taken by the people who have always found it difficult to access the labour market, particularly those living in deprived neighbourhoods.

Most poor people live in neighbourhoods that, at best, are under pressure and need significant change; at worst, they live in neighbourhoods that are failing. The link between failing neighbourhoods and poverty is well-established – in our most deprived neighbourhoods, 1 in 4 adults are out of work and 3 out of 5 people of working age have no, or only minimal, qualifications.

The National Strategy for Neighbourhood Renewal Action Plan, published in 2001, concluded that 2,000 neighbourhoods across England were falling behind the rest, in terms of health, community safety, education, employment and housing. 1 in 6 people were living in these neighbourhoods. Something radical clearly had to be done to turn them round.

Not all these neighbourhoods were failing; many were simply not doing as well as the rest and needed new types of intervention to put them back on their feet. But there was an explicit recognition that past policies and initiatives had largely failed to make a significant impact on the problems. Deprived neighbourhoods were not being turned round despite significant investment programmes through a wide range of predominantly area-based initiatives.

So what has been going wrong? Why have some previously stable neighbourhoods begun to fail? Some of the well-documented factors can be summarised as follows:

- Neighbourhoods have become **more transient and less stable**. All neighbourhoods change over time, but we now live in a highly mobile society, where a complex web of rapidly changing national and international interrelationships can and do have remarkably quick impacts on local neighbourhoods.
- Some urban neighbourhoods with racially mixed communities suffer from a **lack of community cohesion**. Small communities often feel isolated; they frequently cluster together in adjacent streets and racism is a daily part of their lives. Where tensions have boiled over, disturbances have set back renewal programmes, and undermined trust and confidence between communities, entrenching division rather than building cohesion.
- **Household composition has changed** significantly and household numbers are growing rapidly. Many more of us now live on our own – either through choice or relationship breakdown; older people are living longer and need more care;

adult children are living at home well into their twenties as the costs of independence increases. The old notion of a typical 2+2 household is no longer appropriate – households are more diverse and complex than they have ever been, something not always matched by the housing stock itself in many neighbourhoods.

- Household change has led to **lower population densities**; many neighbourhoods have become 'thinner', with less informal interaction between people and an increased use of cars for even the shortest journeys. Increasingly sophisticated, but remote, forms of communication have also made a contribution to greater social isolation, insecurity and fear of crime.

- The **loss of many manual, low-skilled jobs**, or their transfer to remote places, has left many neighbourhoods without a purpose or a solid income base and with low expectations, particularly among young people. Lack of opportunity and the often complete absence of suitable places to meet and interact have contributed to neighbourhood tensions and instability.

- **Young people's aspirations** have also changed. In some northern parts of England many first-time buyers are no longer prepared to accept an older terrace house as a starter home, leaving previously stable neighbourhoods vulnerable to investment landlords and their often associated problems of poor tenancy management and anti-social behaviour.

To these can be added a number of other interrelated factors associated with decline in some of our poorest neighbourhoods:

- Increasing drug-dealing and use
- A predominance of single tenure and single dwelling type estates
- The lack of coordinated, long-term investment in the physical, social and community infrastructure, coupled with inappropriate funding regimes
- Unfocused, uncoordinated and under-managed local services
- An absence of robust and sustained community organisation at neighbourhood level. There is often no-one to champion the neighbourhood's cause, and insufficient resources for community development support
- Tensions between different communities competing for a limited range of neighbourhood resources and facilities
- A poor external image generated by one-off events, adverse publicity and a poor quality environment.

There are clearly many complex and interrelated factors affecting neighbourhood stability. Together, they are capable of tipping many neighbourhoods into decline and, in some cases, failure.

Housing market renewal pathfinders

In housing market renewal pathfinder areas, some neighbourhoods have arguably reached a 'tipping point', after which no reasonable amount of external intervention in the physical and social infrastructure is likely to be successful. Undermined by a weak local economy, many of the pathfinders have concluded that parts of their 'patch' have reached this point and have put forward plans for extensive redevelopment, often in the face of considerable community opposition.

It is worth exploring briefly how perceptions about failing neighbourhoods differ between those charged with renewing housing markets and those communities that are directly affected. The list below is inevitably only a snapshot.

Different perceptions about housing market renewal in failing neighbourhoods

Local authorities/pathfinders	Local communities
What are the issues?	
• Failing housing market • Changing aspirations/falling demand • Low levels of owner occupation • Outdated housing stock and street pattern • Uncoordinated public services • A weak local economy	• Important low-income, affordable housing market • Recent rising house values • Concentration of anti-social households • Protection of neighbourhood and Victorian terrace heritage • Poor quality local services • Lack of local jobs and training, especially for young people
Who is to blame?	
• The market	• The local authority • The government • Private landlords
What should be done?	
• Neighbourhood management • A mix of clearance and refurbishment • Create a more mixed income community • Selective landlord licensing	• Neighbourhood management • Investment in existing homes • Keep existing community together • Compulsory landlord licensing

In some of these neighbourhoods (though certainly not all), local communities accept that there are serious problems and want urgent action to deal with them, but they have a rather different perspective on the nature of the problem and the best ways of tackling it.

They tend to reject the notion that the root cause is an over-supply of outdated terrace housing, placing the blame for neighbourhood decline firmly on the local authority, the loss of job opportunities, the activities of private investment landlords and the associated arrival of anti-social people. *'It's a people, not a housing problem'* is a frequently-heard view. Residents often feel that their neighbourhood has been abandoned by the local authority, after years of neglect, which they are now trying to redress by the blunt instrument of clearance and redevelopment. Residents usually do, however, have a strong view on the importance of neighbourhood management, something they see as more important than physical change.

As ever, it's a mixed picture – no two housing market renewal neighbourhoods are the same and nor are the views of the communities within them. It would also be a mistake to suggest that the government's housing market renewal programme is essentially about large-scale clearance – in practice, the opposite is the case. It is, however, significant that Communities and Local Government's guidance to HMR pathfinders now places a stronger emphasis on securing majority community support for clearance proposals before it will support them, reflecting the wider policy imperatives of the Local Government White Paper 2006.

Community Engagement in Housing-Led Regeneration is a CIH good practice guide which disseminates some of the lessons learned from the experience of the HMR pathfinders.

Estates in decline

Beyond neighbourhoods predominantly comprising older privately-owned terrace homes, major change has been under way on many low-demand estates managed by social landlords up and down the country. Neighbourhoods have arguably failed here not because of the market, but because of the lack of one. Many large, single tenure estates suffering years of under-investment have seen abandonment of the least popular stock.

For local authorities and stock transfer associations, the initial solutions to these problems have centred on a mixture of public and private reinvestment, selective clearance and redevelopment to change the housing mix and tenure. Although this has sometimes led to community opposition, securing major physical change has usually been easier to achieve here than it has been in predominantly private sector older housing neighbourhoods.

Agencies involved in these types of initiatives have also become acutely aware of the need to learn the lessons of the past and ensure that neighbourhood investment is successful in the long term. So alongside the physical investment have come major commitments to strengthening local communities, the social infrastructure and the management of local services. Strengthening local economies is always an important strategic objective but it has, in recent years, lost much of the neighbourhood dimension which was built up, in particular, through the 1990s Single Regeneration Budget programme. This is an issue that needs to be revisited as part of the future agenda for neighbourhoods.

Reversing the trend

Neighbourhoods cannot be turned round overnight – it takes many years of intensive effort and even then there are no guarantees of success. Recent research for the Joseph Rowntree Foundation suggests that neighbourhoods with particularly high levels of deprivation need intensive help to reach a 'take-off' point before people with higher incomes and more choice will move in and help sustain them. If this does not happen, neighbourhoods are likely to become trapped in a cycle of deprivation which becomes more and more difficult to break out of.

The resources required to achieve this are significant and not always available. The research also concluded that there must be a direct link between neighbourhood investment and local labour market policies – raising skill levels among existing residents in deprived neighbourhoods and offering incentives for already skilled people to make their homes there.

Despite these reservations, there is a growing recognition that, given the right ingredients and sufficient time and resources, it is possible to turn round almost any failing neighbourhood. The rest of this chapter looks at the main ingredients for making a neighbourhood successful, and at what is needed to ensure it stays that way.

Renewing failing estates
PLYMOUTH GROVE, MANCHESTER

Plymouth Grove is an innovative Private Finance Initiative which is transforming a once deprived and failing local authority housing estate on the edge of the city centre, into a vibrant, well managed, mixed tenure neighbourhood.

With 1,100 homes in 2003 and laid out in typical 1960s Radburn style, the estate was becoming increasingly unpopular, with high levels of crime, empty homes and turnover.

→

A PFI was drawn up to transform the neighbourhood, with a consortium known as Grove Village, involving Harvest Housing Group, MJ Gleeson Group and Nationwide appointed to take it forward.

Following consultation with residents, 40% of the homes were demolished and the remaining 663 homes were comprehensively refurbished. The estate layout was changed, new roads and footpaths have been constructed and a range of other environmental improvements completed.

Over 650 new homes are being built for sale and will be fully integrated into the existing estate. Restrictive covenants on the new homes prevent investors from letting the houses irresponsibly, with various financial schemes set up to encourage local people to buy in the area.

The consortium has taken over day-to-day management of the neighbourhood, but the city council continues to own the rented homes. Tenants stay as council tenants and keep all their rights. Harvest Housing Group provides neighbourhood management to all households irrespective of tenure. Local residents have been involved from the beginning of the project, in particular at monthly monitoring panel meetings. A separate residents' committee meets with the Grove Village consortium on a regular basis.

Successful neighbourhoods – the main factors

Successful neighbourhoods depend on many things, but conventional wisdom suggests that four ingredients are essential in deprived communities:

- A well-maintained physical environment
- A buoyant local economy
- A robust social infrastructure
- An active, cohesive and fully-engaged community.

The main factors for successful neighbourhoods listed in the table opposite expand on these four themes. They parallel Communities and Local Government's guidance on sustainable communities, but relate it firmly to the neighbourhood agenda. They will not all be appropriate for every neighbourhood.

SUCCESSFUL NEIGHBOURHOODS

KEY FACTORS

- A physically integrated mix of housing tenures, offering a range of genuinely affordable options for people. Poor quality neighbourhoods with a high proportion of social renting and particularly private renting are less likely to be successful in the long term without significant tenure change and a more diverse mix of incomes.

- A range of adaptable house types and sizes, capable of meeting local community needs for the foreseeable future.

- A good quality, well-designed housing stock with regular, ongoing investment in maintenance by both private owners and social landlords.

- A good quality, safe and well-maintained environment.

- Effective democratic neighbourhood representation.

- Active neighbourhood management, with direct involvement of the community in decision-making about local services and a commitment to joined-up operating by service providers.

- Community control of appropriate neighbourhood assets.

- A well-developed social network, with ongoing investment in strengthening and widening social capital.

- A good degree of social cohesion between different communities living alongside each other.

- A clear sense of neighbourhood identity and belonging.

- Good access to essential community facilities for all age groups.

- Access to good schools and employment opportunities.

- Low levels of crime, drugs and anti-social behaviour, with visible and effective neighbourhood policing.

- A good, affordable public transport service, encouraging people to make some journeys without using their cars.

- Demonstrable, year-on-year improvements in the statistical indicators of deprivation – ill health, mortality, worklessness, illiteracy and school performance.

These closely interrelated ingredients are not easy to achieve and many of them require major investment. There are sometimes other, often overlooked, ingredients that can make the biggest difference. Three that stand out are neighbourhood history, neighbourhood pride and neighbourhood leadership.

Neighbourhood history

Neighbourhoods are constantly changing and many of them have an interesting and unique history – in some cases a long one. In many deprived communities this is frequently rooted in the growth and decline of local industry. Many older residents have important memories; they include shared activities, prominent individuals and formerly important buildings. These memories are often rekindled by young people undertaking school projects about their neighbourhood and its history.

Some older buildings are part of a community's roots. Local morale – a key factor in neighbourhood stability – can be boosted if redundant buildings with positive local historic significance are retained and new uses found for them.

Neighbourhood pride

Successful neighbourhoods have a clear, positive identity which is shared by most residents. The 'feel-good' factor is very important in neighbourhoods. People need to feel positive about where they live; too often they feel embarrassed when they tell others about their neighbourhood and many are reluctant to invite friends to their homes.

Neighbourhood pride is a product of many things: a shared history, a collective effort to take responsibility for some aspects of community life or even a successful campaign for change. It is not dependent on outside intervention – it comes from within. Building social capital and cohesion are important milestones in any neighbourhood's progress towards success and ultimate sustainability, but having a basic pride in where you live is an essential starting point. It doesn't necessarily take much to stimulate – finding the right launch pad is often all it needs.

Neighbourhood leadership

Many of the neighbourhoods that have moved from failure to success have benefited from strong and visionary local leadership. These people have often made the crucial difference when external intervention and large-scale resources have been targeted at a failing neighbourhood. Sometimes they have been responsible for securing the resources in the first place.

Neighbourhood leaders can be individual residents or a small group and occasionally an independent outsider. They help to focus residents' agendas for change, build positive, robust relationships with external agencies and act as local champions.

Neighbourhood leaders have a different role from local councillors, focusing on participative rather than representative democracy, but they do have a distinct neighbourhood legitimacy. Unfortunately, they remain a rarity; too many neighbourhoods lack leadership, rely too heavily on external support and never become self-propelled. In other neighbourhoods, momentum has been lost when a particular leader has moved away.

Successful neighbourhoods need reinvigorating from time to time; they have cycles of community strength and leadership. Their long-term success often depends, at least in part, on having a broad community base that is regularly refreshed. There is more about this issue in chapter 6.

Towards more cohesive neighbourhoods

If there is one issue that stands out in recent discussions about successful neighbourhoods it is community cohesion. Although the degree of 'cohesiveness' will vary significantly from one neighbourhood to another, cohesive neighbourhoods can be identified in general terms as ones where:

- There is a common vision and a sense of belonging for everyone in the local community
- The diversity of people's different backgrounds and circumstances is appreciated and positively valued
- Those from different backgrounds, races and faiths have similar life opportunities
- Strong and positive relationships are being developed between people from different backgrounds and circumstances in the workplace, in schools and through a variety of neighbourhood and community networks.

So community cohesion, although at present primarily associated, by government, with ethnicity and/or faith, has a broader dimension. It is about bringing everyone in a neighbourhood together in ways that promote harmony, a good quality of life and new opportunities for all residents – by no means an easy thing to achieve in any neighbourhood, but hugely important nevertheless.

Britain today has 60 million people, speaking over 300 different languages and practising at least 14 different faiths. It could and should be a richly diverse and stable society. However, diversity seems to be dividing communities in some places. It was the succession of largely inner city riots in the early 1980s and then in 2001 that focused minds on the importance of bringing people from different backgrounds together in neighbourhoods and not pursuing policies and initiatives that, perhaps inadvertently, drove them apart. A more recent dimension is the arrival of new migrants from the EU accession states.

Following the 2001 riots, and an influential report by Ted Cantle, the government set up a community cohesion pathfinder programme which aimed to test and evaluate new methods of developing social cohesion and community participation in a wide range of different communities across the country. There were 14 pathfinder areas covering 23 local authorities. They lasted for 18 months and led directly to the publication of a practitioners' toolkit on how to deliver community cohesion in neighbourhoods.

In June 2006, the government set up the Commission on Integration and Cohesion. Due to report in June 2007, the terms of reference include:

- Examining the issues that raise tensions between different groups in different areas, and that lead to segregation and conflict
- Suggesting how local community and political leadership can push further against perceived barriers to cohesion and integration
- Looking at how local communities themselves can be empowered to tackle extremist ideologies
- Developing approaches that build local areas' own capacity to prevent problems, and ensure they have the structures in place to recover from periods of tension.

The Chartered Institute of Housing has published two guides on this subject, setting out what housing providers can do to contribute to greater community cohesion. How this can help to create and sustain successful neighbourhoods is set out in chapter 7.

COMMUNITY COHESION

THE BENEFITS AND RISKS TO NEIGHBOURHOODS

The main benefits of more cohesive neighbourhoods

- Less crime, anti-social behaviour, racist harassment and neighbour disputes
- A more stable housing market, with lower household turnover
- Greater resident involvement in local community networks, with more self-help
- More ethnically mixed schools, health and leisure facilities
- Enriched experiences for residents, through greater social mixing and respect for diversity.

The risks for less-cohesive neighbourhoods

- A negative image of the neighbourhood, creating isolation and a 'siege' mentality
- Falling demand and abandonment of homes
- Paralysis in the delivery of regeneration and renewal programmes
- Riots and disturbances
- Segregated local community facilities, reinforcing disadvantage, mistrust and rumour, duplicating revenue-intensive services and fuelling inter-community resentment.

Community-led neighbourhood management

BALSALL HEATH NEIGHBOURHOOD FORUM, BIRMINGHAM

Balsall Heath Neighbourhood Forum is one of the country's pioneers of community-led neighbourhood management. Over the years it has been quietly enabling more and more local people to improve the quality of their lives in a formerly notorious inner city area of Birmingham that for many years was dominated by the prostitution industry.

Balsall Heath is a neighbourhood with a high level of cultural and ethnic diversity, but, until recently, many people lived out their lives in isolation from their neighbours. It was a relatively weak neighbourhood in need of a kick-start. The Forum has been the key to putting Balsall Heath back on track.

The Forum is a community-controlled company, with 18 elected resident members. It represents the voice of local people to both the public and private sectors and, from the start, has set about rearranging the way Balsall Heath is managed and governed.

The Forum does five things:

1. Represents the views of local people to those in authority.
2. Rebuilds social infrastructure through developing voluntary and faith groups.
3. Delivers services to improve the local environment (eg involvement in the Cleaner and Greener initiative and winning 'Britain in Bloom').
4. Develops and delivers neighbourhood management plans.
5. Exports principles of how and how not to do things and disseminates what it does well, as part of the Guide Neighbourhoods programme.

Balsall Heath Neighbourhood Forum is keen to expand its role by securing the transfer of public assets, to itself and other voluntary organisations it works with. It also has aspirations with its partners to form a new registered social landlord, which would enable the local community to control the management and maintenance of the council housing in Balsall Heath – seen as a source of continuing problems.

How successful neighbourhoods can sustain themselves

Neighbourhoods change constantly, some faster than others. The key to sustainability is to detect change early and take action to mitigate its worst effects, be able to manage it effectively when it comes, and at a pace that fits with community and external expectations.

Time-limited investment programmes have some value for turning failing neighbourhoods round, but the resources are often wasted if there are no plans for what happens at the end of the initiative. The succession strategies for government programmes like New Deal for Communities are crucially important, just as they were for the Housing Action Trusts and many of the Single Regeneration Budget programmes that preceded them.

Recent research (see chapter 7 for more details) suggests that the commitment to breaking up historic mono-tenure patterns on large estates and creating more mixed-income communities has been reasonably successful. However, diversifying tenure and incomes will not necessarily bring lasting change. Households move in and out of neighbourhoods for many reasons and most are more mobile than they were in the past. There is, therefore, a danger that, as individuals move, old tenure patterns may begin to reappear, with much of the good work of the recent past reversed. The longer-term success of neighbourhoods is likely to depend rather more on the quality of the environment, local school performance, how much wealth is circulating in the local economy and crime and safety issues.

Climate change and policy responses to it are likely to have an increasing impact on neighbourhoods. The next decades will see measures to reduce private car use, the building of eco-homes, improved thermal insulation of existing homes to reduce energy use and tackle fuel poverty, more use of neighbourhood combined heat and power schemes, solar panels and wind generators and more efficient waste recycling. The impact of these changes on many places may be significant; carbon-neutral neighbourhoods are just round the corner, while some popular low-lying coastal neighbourhoods may even need to be abandoned altogether as sea levels rise.

One of the key measures to keep neighbourhoods successful is neighbourhood management. Most neighbourhoods need to be actively managed over the long term, whether or not they are successful, to tackle these and other difficulties. For many this may be little more than a light touch; for others something more intensive will be required. Neighbourhoods need to be constantly monitored and the resources applied to them adjusted as circumstances change, something that has been missing from neighbourhood policy so far.

CHAPTER 5

MAKING IT HAPPEN: NEIGHBOURHOOD MANAGEMENT

This chapter focuses on how to manage neighbourhoods successfully. It looks at the roll out of neighbourhood management across England, drawing on recent evaluations to show what works. It then considers how this fits with the new agenda outlined in the previous chapters, focusing on what needs to be done to embed neighbourhood management as the most effective way of ensuring our neighbourhoods meet local aspirations and offer long-term quality of life to their residents.

Neighbourhood management was seen as one of the key planks of the government's National Strategy for Neighbourhood Renewal when it was first launched in 2001. It was a largely untried and certainly untested approach. Several years on, it has now become the main vehicle for delivering the neighbourhood agenda across the country, with 35 government-sponsored neighbourhood management pathfinders and more than 200 other initiatives now up and running. Almost all of them are performing well; neighbourhood management is clearly making a difference. It is arguably *the* key tool for keeping low-income neighbourhoods successful.

Despite these successes, neighbourhood management is by no means universally applied. Many local authorities and service agencies remain somewhat sceptical about it and even more communities have yet to encounter it. While some of the barriers are significant, there is little doubt that the potential benefits of neighbourhood management are enough to overcome them.

The main benefits of neighbourhood management

- Improving local service delivery
- Encouraging and underpinning active and engaged communities
- Strengthening the local democratic process
- Delivering local authority and service providers' priorities
- Promoting joined-up working between service providers and communities
- Reducing levels of deprivation in neighbourhoods
- Making things happen.

The main barriers to neighbourhood management

- It is not an easy option
- Joined-up working between service providers is improving, but not yet fully embedded
- There is fragmentation of responsibilities for neighbourhood renewal, social inclusion and community development within local authorities
- Some professionals, agencies and politicians are still reluctant to give up power, influence and particularly budgets
- There are tensions between neighbourhood priorities and the strategic aims of service providers
- There is a culture of dependency among neighbourhood residents – many still feel it's the council's job to sort everything out
- There may be a shortage of active residents to drive neighbourhood management
- There is often a breakdown in trust between residents and service providers.

Neighbourhood management – the essential elements

Six years' experience of neighbourhood management and two rounds of evaluation of the national pathfinders have helped to identify the key elements required:

- *A clearly defined neighbourhood*
- *Resident involvement*
- *A dynamic neighbourhood manager, with clout*
- *A local partnership and an anchor organisation to provide strategic direction*
- *Understanding, support and commitment from the local authority and local strategic partnership, including financial commitment*
- *Quality information*
- *Commitment from service providers and mechanisms for engagement between providers and residents.*

A clearly defined neighbourhood

Despite the difficulties of definition, referred to in chapter 1, managing neighbourhoods successfully depends on focusing activity within clearly defined boundaries. The size of a neighbourhood is also important. The evaluation of the neighbourhood management pathfinders has found that the costs per head of population tend to increase in areas below 5,000, and that residents are unlikely to identify as a neighbourhood an area of more than 15,000 people, even in the most intensively built-up area.

Nevertheless, there are some good examples of successful neighbourhood management in much smaller neighbourhoods – particularly, but not exclusively in rural areas – and it is clear that there is no standard approach to neighbourhood management.

Resident involvement

Neighbourhood management depends on the direct involvement of local communities. Significant amounts of time, effort and resources are needed to support and sustain different levels of resident involvement at different stages, in order to:

- Support residents' direct involvement on a local partnership board and in working groups
- Support and develop community leaders or champions
- Support neighbourhood-based community organisations
- Reach out to residents not involved in organisations
- Identify and reach out to those people who face barriers to getting involved.

A dynamic neighbourhood manager with clout

Neighbourhood managers are important individuals; they need to have the authority to take an overview of service delivery, to coordinate the various providers and be able to negotiate for change both locally and, just as importantly, at a senior level. So the best neighbourhood managers are not necessarily tried and trusted area housing managers with a new job title and job description. They must have clout well beyond the neighbourhood; they must be people who others will listen to.

As well has having the right qualities, the neighbourhood manager needs a team, working from a base in the neighbourhood. Local circumstances will dictate the size and composition. The team will usually include deliverers of services who may be employed by, loaned or seconded to the partnership.

A local partnership, to provide strategic direction

Some form of partnership structure is needed to provide strategic direction and leadership for neighbourhood management. Ideally the partnership will bring together residents, local councillors and key service providers. Those on the partnership executive need the ability to think and act strategically, grasp the neighbourhood management concept, be committed to delivering it, and, crucially, have the authority to make strategic, policy and resource decisions.

The neighbourhood management pathfinders have all developed partnership boards. These may be unincorporated or incorporated – the latter is important if the partnership is going to employ its own staff, own assets or let contracts. Some neighbourhood management pathfinder boards have resident majorities, something which gives communities real power over their neighbourhoods, often for the first time. There is more on this later in the chapter.

Support and commitment from the local authority and Local Strategic Partnership

The local partnership will need to develop good links with local authority-wide structures, particularly with the local authority itself and Local Strategic Partnership (LSP). In two-tier authorities this will mean setting up and maintaining good links with both district and county authorities and LSPs. Developing good relationships with local councillors is also very important.

Quality information

A key task of any neighbourhood management partnership is to collect and analyse good quality baseline and monitoring information on:

- Neighbourhood conditions
- Residents' needs and priorities
- Evidence for change
- The effects of interventions and doing things differently.

A mixture of qualitative and quantitative information is needed. 'Soft' information about people's perceptions, feelings and opinions are just as important as hard information. There have been major improvements in statistical provision, including the Neighbourhood Statistics website, but getting hold of quality information at neighbourhood level remains problematic sometimes.

Commitment from service providers and mechanisms for engagement between providers and residents

Service providers need to be committed to the principles and aims of neighbourhood management, promote cultural change within their staff teams and organisations and be highly receptive to new ways of thinking. This commitment needs to be demonstrated at local, middle and senior management levels.

Structures and mechanisms should be developed that provide residents with a means of challenging service providers, agreeing levels of service and holding service providers to account through a range of mechanisms, including the new community calls for action process.

The pathfinder experience

At the time of writing, the government's neighbourhood management pathfinder programme has been running for more than four years, with 20 first round initiatives, mainly led by local authorities in urban areas, and 15 second round initiatives, some based in rural areas and led by a more mixed group of service providers, including housing associations.

All the pathfinders are being supported by public funding of between £350,000 and £500,000 a year. This includes core costs as well as money for testing out new ways of doing things. At between £10 and £40 per person per year, this makes neighbourhood management a relatively low-cost programme, certainly when compared with the huge investment in neighbourhood renewal.

Despite this, there is already some scepticism about whether neighbourhood management can be rolled out more widely without a significant national budget. A number of local authorities and some service providers are now running neighbourhood management programmes without this level of public funding support but, as the following section highlights, there are doubts that some of the lessons from the pathfinder programme have really been learned.

Four key success factors stand out within the Round 1 pathfinders:
- *Analysis, learning and action:* identifying priority needs, enabling and prompting service providers to address needs in a much more systematic way
- *Leadership, management and champions:* creating strategic direction and leadership through partnership boards, a neighbourhood management team and networking via theme groups
- *Service level agreements, protocols and other formalities:* to embed service improvements and offer redress to neighbourhood communities for under-performance
- *Engagement of residents and communities:* to bring them to the heart of decisions about neighbourhood services.

Neighbourhood management is more about reorganising the way things are done than inventing new and costly ways of working, but it would be a mistake to believe it can be done 'on the cheap'. Significant, regular and long-term investment will always be needed.

The pathfinder experience certainly provides important pointers to good practice. The following sections set out four of the main lessons learned so far.

Not all service providers are yet signed up to the neighbourhood management approach

The table below uses information drawn from the ongoing evaluation of the Round 1 pathfinders in 2005/06. Among other things, it shows that, in most cases, the police, Primary Care Trusts, local schools and local authority housing and environmental services have been the easiest partners to engage and that housing associations are strengthening their involvement, but in most cases have not been core supporters. A number of service providers remain fringe players.

Level of involvement	Service provider	Change between 2004 and 2005
'Core supporters'	Police Primary Care Trusts Local schools Council housing services Environmental services	No change Stronger Stronger Stronger No change
'Friends, but not always close'	Job Centre Plus Council youth services Council leisure services Housing associations	Stronger Stronger No change Stronger
'Acquaintances'	Local colleges Connexions Fire service	Weaker No change Stronger
'Strangers'	National Offender Management Service Learning and Skills Councils Public transport bodies Council social services	No change No change No change No change

The delivery of most mainstream public services in neighbourhoods has improved as a direct result of neighbourhood management. In general terms, neighbourhood services have become (in order of most change):

- More responsive to local needs
- Provided in greater quantity
- More accessible
- Higher quality
- Better targeted
- More efficient.

Policing has become more responsive, with more activity on the ground

The police have been at the forefront of the neighbourhood management agenda since its inception. The level of 'bobbies on the beat' has increased and stronger links have been established with local communities. New local bases have been established and joint working to tackle anti-social behaviour has proved successful.

These improvements are not all down to a neighbourhood management approach within the pathfinders; they also reflect a national move towards neighbourhood policing. Nevertheless, other service providers have much to learn from the enthusiasm and commitment that the police have shown to the neighbourhood agenda. There is more about neighbourhood policing later in this chapter.

The involvement of housing providers has strengthened

Nevertheless, most remain more focused on investment, redevelopment and stock transfers than on localising and devolving responsibility for the housing management service. See chapter 7 for more on this.

The most important changes in environmental services have been improved integration and efficiency

This is particularly true of street cleaning, waste collection and grounds maintenance, with related rises in resident satisfaction.

Safe and clean

GREATER LEVER NEIGHBOURHOOD MANAGEMENT PATHFINDER, BOLTON

Greater Lever is a largely residential, ethnically mixed suburb of Bolton. The pathfinder has developed charters to formalise agreements on neighbourhood service standards, covering response times, targets and resources.

Residents identified crime and street cleaning as early priorities for action. The Safe and Clean Charter was developed through negotiations between residents, the police and Bolton MBC with the overall objective to *'address the quality of the physical environment and to focus on both the physical and social impact of crime and anti-social behaviour.'*

The Charter sets out clear targets and the resources available, what each service provider is responsible for, what level of service the community can expect from individual providers, key service contacts, information about specific initiatives in the pathfinder area and clear monitoring arrangements.

→

The Charter has become a working tool against which services are measured. It has clearly strengthened neighbourhood service delivery and multi-agency working in Greater Lever.

The Safe and Clean Charter has had a measurable impact since it was introduced. Reported burglaries have fallen, Greater Lever is now a much cleaner place and there has been a significant increase in the number of people who like living in the area, from 61% in a 2003 community survey, to 71% in 2006.

Mainstreaming neighbourhood management

The pathfinders have shown that neighbourhood management can be a key factor – perhaps the key factor – in neighbourhood success. But, however successful they are, 35 pathfinders, covering 150,000 homes, will have only a small impact on delivering the neighbourhood agenda across the country. The approach needs to be rolled out much more widely.

To some extent this is already beginning to happen. There are more than 200 neighbourhood management initiatives around the country outside the pathfinder programme. All the local authorities with pathfinders have been convinced enough by their success to spread the experience to other neighbourhoods, and many of the local authorities receiving Neighbourhood Element money through Local Area Agreements are developing neighbourhood management.

But approaches vary. Some local authorities are rolling out a version of neighbourhood management across much larger areas than the pathfinders are covering – with delivery responsibility delegated to area committees or boards. This is area, rather than neighbourhood, management. Other local authorities are replicating the pathfinder model in a second neighbourhood, albeit with fewer resources. In most cases, however, there is a recognition that the key principles of neighbourhood management should apply across the borough as a whole.

The cost of neighbourhood management lies at the heart of the dilemma about how it could and should be rolled out more widely. Comprehensive neighbourhood management approaches are seen by some local authorities as too costly and unsustainable. In some ways this may seem surprising; neighbourhood management is relatively cheap, compared to other neighbourhood-based initiatives. Nevertheless, financial pressures are undoubtedly a significant restraining factor. Mainstreaming finance as a core part of budgets is essential.

MAINSTREAMING NEIGHBOURHOOD MANAGEMENT IN SALFORD

Salford City Council delivers its comprehensive neighbourhood management programme through community committees across all eight areas of the city. The approach, which has been in place for three years, has its roots in the city-wide Community Strategy that was developed in 1995.

The community committees are made up of local councillors and members of community and voluntary groups. Each has developed a Community Action Plan covering health, crime, learning and leisure, young people, inclusion, life enhancement and prosperity.

Each community committee is supported by its own neighbourhood management team. In most areas this consists of a neighbourhood manager, community development worker and administrator. A wider team of staff from partner agencies and council directorates works together under the leadership of the neighbourhood manager to problem-solve and deliver local priorities.

The community committees all have devolved budgets, currently based on £2.30 per head of population. They use this to help deliver the priorities set out in the Community Action Plans, by commissioning services and targeting funding at key initiatives as well as supporting local organisations.

Around £100,000 mainstream funding from the Highways Department has also been allocated to each area to be spent locally and there are plans to include Section 106 (planning gain) funding from developers in the devolved arrangements.

Plans for the future include piloting the local scrutiny of services, developing an increased role for children and young people to have their voices heard and targeting resources on the most disadvantaged communities to promote a step change in outcomes for residents in these areas.

Future resourcing will depend on where neighbourhood management sits within Local Area Agreements. Although there are some early encouraging signs, particularly in terms of local empowerment and joining up services, there are also the concerns about cost. Cash-strapped local authorities may feel that roll out over larger areas (of more than 15,000 people) might provide economies of scale. It is an attractive, but potentially flawed approach:

- Watering down neighbourhood management, by taking a 'pick and mix' approach to delivery, will inevitably weaken its impact

- Recent research suggests that few economies of scale can be achieved if neighbourhood management is rolled out to areas with populations of more than 15,000

- These larger areas are not neighbourhoods, so there is the risk of losing many of the benefits of focusing on places that communities identify with.

Other factors which may constrain mainstreaming include:

- Difficulties in securing cultural change among providers. Some services have changed their processes permanently as a result of neighbourhood management, some are in the process of doing so and others have yet to start. Continual support and pressure is needed.

- Problems recruiting experienced neighbourhood management staff.

- Political sensitivities about investment priorities between competing neighbourhoods.

MAINSTREAMING NEIGHBOURHOOD MANAGEMENT IN WOLVERHAMPTON

The City of Wolverhampton has developed seven neighbourhood management pilots and is now planning to roll out the approach across the city, to bring it into the mainstream of planning and service delivery. This process has been a focus of recent national evaluation research. The Local Strategic Partnership, and its many connections with service providers, has been a key driver of the neighbourhood management pilots.

Wolverhampton has a history of area networks, established in the 1990s through European funding. The neighbourhood management pilots were a natural extension of this approach. Each employs a neighbourhood manager and a neighbourhood team. The scheme also draws upon 'natural boundaries', moving away from political wards. These natural boundaries are now officially recognised by statutory services as well as local people.

Each neighbourhood team has delegated funding and is encouraged to look for additional resources. Each works to its own annual action plan, focusing on the needs and aspirations of local people, and has a local board made up of representatives from community service providers and local businesses.

The local authority has been closely monitoring progress on the initiative, to develop and broaden political support for the project. With this political support in place, the project has now been rolled out across the city, significantly changing the way mainstream services are delivered city-wide as well at a local level.

Although the pathfinder model was never intended to be rigidly adopted elsewhere, there are strong arguments against watering down the approach and losing the tight neighbourhood focus. Rolling out into successive deprived neighbourhoods may therefore make more sense than early mainstreaming across a borough at a lower and less effective level. But circumstances are different in every area; feasibility work to establish the best approach will always be helpful.

As always, the setting and meeting of targets is a crucial element in gaining ongoing support and funding through Local Area Agreements, Local Strategic Partnerships and local authorities, something which will be closely monitored by government offices.

NEIGHBOURHOOD MANAGEMENT – WHERE NEXT?
POTENTIAL CRITERIA FOR CHOOSING THE RIGHT NEIGHBOURHOOD

- **Strategic 'fit':** neighbourhoods where the maximum impact can be achieved, with potential for bringing in additional resources through a range of programmes
- **Resources for physical renewal**, to complement neighbourhood management activities and deliver comprehensive change
- **Established need:** neighbourhoods where deprivation is concentrated – usually within the top 20% of nationally deprived wards
- **Community pressure for change:** neighbourhoods where residents are dissatisfied with local services
- **Neighbourhoods with clearly defined boundaries**, which the local community can identify with
- **The potential for early change**, not a neighbourhood needing major investment with no early prospect of significant resources
- **Prevention rather than reaction**, focusing on neighbourhoods where there has been little past investment and where there is a need to prevent problems getting worse rather than reacting to deep-seated problems
- **Prevention with reaction**, focusing on a neighbourhood with deep-seated problems which has failed to respond despite significant past investment and needs a fresh approach
- **Service providers' priorities:** neighbourhoods where local providers feel they need or want to focus on
- **Improving the image:** neighbourhoods which are important for the image of the town or city and which, if significantly improved, would have important spin-offs
- **Political support**, for targeting resources on specific neighbourhoods; not spreading the jam too thinly.

For mainstreaming neighbourhood management to succeed it is important to learn from experience so far, via the recent evaluation of the pathfinders and also the more qualitative experience of practitioners. Some of the less tangible success factors which are critical to the successful extension of neighbourhood management beyond pilot areas are summarised below.

NEIGHBOURHOOD MANAGEMENT – WHERE NEXT?
CRITICAL SUCCESS FACTORS

- Finding high calibre neighbourhood managers
- Establishing a close working relationship with the local authority, with access to the highest levels to secure change
- Cementing neighbourhood management in the consciousness of service providers – getting them to create new patterns and repeat them until new habits and ways of working form
- Having time to change things
- Tailoring the approach to local circumstances/issues
- Having a robust approach to social justice as a core work element
- Having a shared understanding of neighbourhood management and agreeing the key principles
- Securing consistent, local political support
- Ensuring housing-led initiatives go beyond 'housing management plus'
- Working through governance issues early and thoroughly
- Addressing issues on participation v representation (ie getting clear understanding and agreement on the roles of councillors and residents and getting shared understanding that these are complementary rather than contradictory or in conflict)
- Mapping resources in the neighbourhood – establishing baselines which are comprehensive and regularly reviewed
- Using participatory evaluation, with help from a critical friend.

Mainstreaming – where does the money come from?

Spreading neighbourhood management more widely is a major challenge, not least because it raises important issues about how much of it can be resourced by juggling existing budgets and how much requires special funding.

Beyond the pathfinders, much will depend on the ability of Local Strategic Partnerships to access the neighbourhood element of the Safer and Stronger Communities Fund, currently targeted at the 100 most disadvantaged neighbourhoods in England; and the success of funding bids through Local Area Agreements as these are rolled out more widely.

There is unlikely to be any further direct central government funding support; neighbourhood management will increasingly be seen as an activity that could and should be funded from mainstream revenue resources, not special funding. This is not, perhaps, surprising, given that only around 0.2% of all the public funding going into neighbourhoods is needed to core-fund neighbourhood management itself.

Housing providers with significant stock holdings in neighbourhoods have a key role to play in helping resource neighbourhood management. They have a vested interest in ensuring that these neighbourhoods are successful, and neighbourhood management should be a key aspect of their operations, with budget lines in their business plans to support it.

Setting up a delivery body

Different models of neighbourhood management require different methods of delivery in different neighbourhoods. There is no one successful model; nor should there be.

Neighbourhood boards have been the predominant form of delivery vehicle in the pathfinders and they have generally worked well. Residents and service providers are well represented and board membership is generally diverse, as the accompanying pie chart shows.

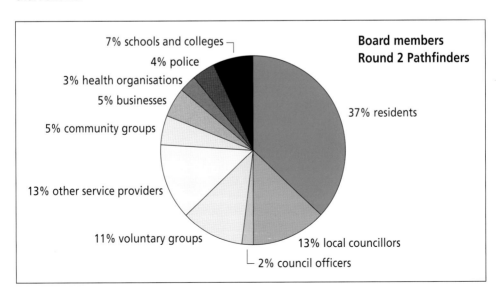

7% schools and colleges
4% police
3% health organisations
5% businesses
5% community groups
13% other service providers
11% voluntary groups
13% local councillors
2% council officers

**Board members
Round 2 Pathfinders**

37% residents

Neighbourhood management boards are not, however, the only way of delivering neighbourhood management. Indeed, the neighbourhood agenda, with its emphasis on governance, holding service providers to account and community asset ownership, suggests that rather different, more robust structures with greater delivery powers may be needed. The extensive menu of options includes:

- **Existing bodies**, where an existing organisation, such as a housing association or voluntary organisation is restructured to enable neighbourhood management to be dealt with separately from its core business.

- **New neighbourhood boards or partnerships**, where residents and service providers are part of a new legally constituted structure at neighbourhood level.

- **A housing regeneration company**, an asset-owning body which links housing renewal with regeneration (it can be structured as a housing association, joint venture company or as an 'arms length' body of the local authority), and provides the opportunity to combine housing management and development with the delivery of other services.

- **A community-based housing organisation**, which can own and/or manage housing stock, is run by the community in which it operates and is usually involved in developing and managing a wide range of community projects alongside its main housing management role, for example, an expanded TMO.

- **A community development or land trust**, community-led bodies with social and economic objectives which can create and own assets and make profits which are re-invested in the community, offering the opportunity for combining social enterprise with service delivery (see chapter 6 for more information).

A housing lead on neighbourhood management
CASTLE VALE COMMUNITY HOUSING ASSOCIATION, BIRMINGHAM

By the early 1990s, Castle Vale was considered one of the most difficult estates in the midlands. A 12 year Housing Action Trust regeneration programme transformed the estate into a popular neighbourhood, where 700 people are queuing up to live.

The transformation continues to be delivered through Castle Vale Community Housing Association (CVCHA), an independent resident-led housing association and a Neighbourhood Partnership Board.

CVCHA provides the hub and infrastructure to deliver a range of non-housing services and regeneration projects. It also hosts the Neighbourhood Partnership Board where CVCHA is an equal partner alongside other statutory providers and residents. As a mainstream housing organisation, the partnership board is backed by an organisation of longstanding in the community – a key factor in neighbourhood sustainability.

→

The Neighbourhood Partnership Board is funded by an endowment made by the HAT. Funding also comes from CVCHA, the local authority, police and the PCT, with each providing £10,000 from mainstream budgets. They can see the benefits and impacts of partnership working in a specific neighbourhood; there is a strong business and community case for its continued support.

CVCHA is part of the Guide Neighbourhoods programme, enabling it to link up with other organisations to share learning and develop strategies to ensure they continue to do things better in Castle Vale. The priority, however, is to develop the skills and approaches in their own community.

These delivery mechanisms offer the potential for neighbourhood management to start at a basic level, with an informal neighbourhood grouping, and progress to a more sophisticated model, such as a community development trust. They will not all be appropriate for every neighbourhood and there are, in any case, pros and cons attached to each of them. The status and prospects of existing structures in the area will clearly be important. Adapting existing structures may be easier than setting up completely new ones.

The need for a strategic framework

Whichever delivery mechanisms are adopted, they all need to operate within a clear strategic framework if neighbourhood management is to become a successful mainstream, rather than one-off, activity. Strategic direction and coordination is needed centrally, particularly in larger towns and cities. Local Strategic Partnerships may have a role to play, although most are not yet delivery-focused, and in many places the strategic role has been carried out by the local authority. Nevertheless, even in rural counties, LSPs can have a key role.

Where area structures exist in cities, they can complement, rather than contradict, neighbourhood management arrangements. The combination of area-based officer resources and area committees with delegated powers and budgets can provide a structure which could be important in the practical development and delivery of neighbourhood management. In the future, area committees may offer direction, support and a troubleshooting role; they could provide advice, support and training to individual neighbourhood management bodies and, potentially, generate revenue to support neighbourhood management in various localities.

How to create and sustain successful neighbourhood partnerships

Public sector organisations in the UK are involved in approximately 5,500 different partnerships, spending or managing just under £4 billion a year. Housing providers are already leading some of these partnerships and contributing to many more. This section draws on the extensive experience across the country to look at the essential ingredients for successful partnerships that can stand the test of time.

Developing effective partnerships

NORTH BENWELL NEIGHBOURHOOD MANAGEMENT PARTNERSHIP NEWCASTLE UPON TYNE

The Neighbourhood Management Initiative (NMI) in North Benwell, Newcastle was set up in 2003, and is led by Home Group, in partnership with Newcastle City Council, Bridging Newcastle/Gateshead Pathfinder and Northumbria Police. The focus of the initiative has been on stabilising and regenerating this ethnically-mixed deprived neighbourhood by reducing the number of empty homes, cutting crime and improving the environment.

The NMI adopted a strong community-led approach from the start. 18 people sit on the Partnership Board, a mixture of residents and agencies. The chairperson is a local resident. Board members have received training on a broad range of partnership development topics, including: setting terms of reference, working together effectively, reviewing the aims and objectives and delivering action on the ground.

The Board meets bi-monthly and has started to take on responsibility for the delivery of certain projects, including development of a Neighbourhood Agreement. Working groups covering youth, housing, the environment and community safety have also been established.

Despite many notable successes, partnerships often fall short of what they should be – practical structures which are about changing things and doing them better. All partnerships run into problems of one sort or another. Where local communities and service providers come together in neighbourhoods, some of the more familiar ones are:

- **Overload** – there are simply too many partnerships, too many meetings, too much consultation and not enough action
- **Tokenism** – community representation is built in because it is *required* rather than *wanted*, with too much reliance on involving the 'usual suspects'
- **Professional territorialism** – joined-up working is, ironically, often at its least evident in partnerships, with each agency hanging on to its territory, funding and resources, offering much, but doing little

- **Cultural barriers** – meetings are too often replicas of local authority committee structures: formal, boring, dominated by jargon and procedural issues, and only comfortable for professionals
- **Resistance to change and sharing information** – too often, professionals want to keep things the way they are, and do so by not sharing information
- **Hidden agendas** – suspicions about hidden agendas in partnerships lead to lack of trust and undermine successful delivery
- **Blame culture** – there is a frequent aversion to risk, too much playing safe and being quick to blame others when things go wrong
- **Cynicism and disillusionment** – both from professionals and communities.

Every member of a neighbourhood partnership should ask themselves three questions before getting involved: what do we want from the partnership, what are we prepared to give, and are we prepared to play a variety of roles that don't necessarily include leadership? If these questions can be answered clearly and honestly, they can provide the basis for effective partnership work between service providers and local communities.

SUCCESSFUL NEIGHBOURHOOD PARTNERSHIPS

Key principles

- **Giving more than taking** – too often partnerships are about status, political preferment and getting hold of more money when they should be about levelling out power imbalances through agencies giving money, time, commitment and resources – 'its about bringing the bottle not fighting for the party bag'.
- **Listening more than talking** – perhaps the hardest thing to do, but has a huge impact in terms of building relationships and developing understanding – 'one of the best ways to persuade others is with your ears'.
- **Respecting and trusting other partners** – community representatives are often exposed to considerable pressures as individuals and representatives, as are some professionals (but at least they get paid for it) – equality, openness and taking time are key elements of building mutual respect and trust.
- **Sharing a common understanding and vision** – the strength of a partnership is that the whole is more than the sum of the individual parts; this can only be achieved through taking time to establish and develop a shared vision, values and language and identifying collective interests and acknowledging inter-dependency.
- **Changing and adapting** – partners must be willing to be influenced as much as they seek to influence; a partnership needs to have a commitment to ongoing learning, the willingness to change and adapt and encourage and respond to criticism.

→

- **Taking responsibility and sharing risk** – collective responsibility and acting for the good of the partnership is vital, as is being creative, experimental and taking risks.
- **Being patient and allowing time** – building a partnership takes considerable time and effort, and needs regular review and change along the way; 30-40 years of problems in communities cannot be turned around in even five years.
- **Inclusivity and accountability** – valuing the contributions of all partners, especially the community, is critical; professionals do not have the monopoly on ideas and methods – 'everyone is ignorant, only on different subjects'.

SUCCESSFUL NEIGHBOURHOOD PARTNERSHIPS

Key requirements

- **Establishing the rules of engagement** – clarity about the roles, responsibilities and contributions of every partner is needed, including a simple terms of reference, code of conduct and information about financial arrangements.
- **Capacity building the partners** – necessary for all, not just the community representatives – some professionals will need help to change from a 'back room' to a 'frontline' approach.
- **Independent resources** – partnerships need resources which are independent from individual partners and to which all have access.
- **Focusing on success** – it is important to identify likely areas of success and work on these first – quick wins are important for the credibility of any partnership.
- **Valuing community involvement** – community involvement must be valued in practical terms by having partnership meetings in community buildings, in the evening, with imaginative approaches to papers and presentations, payment to community representatives and being inclusive, by developing outreach work with 'hard-to-reach' groups.
- **Tiers of involvement** – community representation should take place on different levels, not stop at having a few community representatives on the partnership board – people should be able to choose their level of engagement.
- **Continuous communication** – there should be an ongoing programme of publicity and celebrations about the work of the partnership, both to highlight the work, but also to provide recognition of the individual partners.
- **Consistency and continuity of representation** – it is preferable to have representation that is consistent to encourage trust, shared skills and knowledge, and develop experience. But provision must be made for turnover – people will always leave and move on.

However well a partnership works, it should not be assumed that it will go on indefinitely. One of the problems, however, is that partnerships can run out of steam before they have finished the job. To sustain a neighbourhood partnership which still has a useful life, it is important to:

- Review regularly the vision, objectives and outcomes
- Put in place a performance and risk management plan
- Provide good and regular information to partners and the wider community
- Build the strength of, and trust between, partners, through training, support and socialising
- Build a consensus beyond the partnership to secure long-term political and strategic support
- Keep the community on board, by ensuring that outcomes continually meet residents' needs and expectations
- Recognise when the job is done, agree an appropriate wind-down of activity and hand things over to other appropriate bodies.

Every neighbourhood management initiative needs a simple and motivational performance management system in place for monitoring, evaluating and reviewing partnership development and improvements in service delivery throughout its life. There is more on approaches to evaluation in chapter 7. Monitoring how the partnership is working in practice should involve regular reviews of:

- How the culture of the partnership is changing
- How well the partnership is being governed
- The way local residents and stakeholders are engaged in the process
- How the skills and knowledge of partnership members are developing.

Although neighbourhood management is an ongoing process, not a time-limited activity, many partnerships will undoubtedly need refreshing at some stage. It will be important to ensure that all the benefits of the approach are not lost and that the culture and ethos of neighbourhood service delivery and community engagement are embedded in any future arrangements that emerge.

The changing role of local councillors

Neighbourhood management offers local councillors, particularly those not involved as Executive members, a new role in their political wards, one which is more hands-on, more about community engagement and development and less about formal representation. While requiring a shift in some traditional ways of working, it has the potential to reinvigorate local democracy and with it the political fortunes of many committed individuals.

Councillors need to act as neighbourhood consensus builders, conflict resolvers and facilitators, not just advocates for their community, council or political party. They need to balance their status as democratically elected representatives with a recognition that participatory democracy and working directly with often unelected community representatives on an equal basis, can make all the difference.

Local councillors need to be on neighbourhood management partnerships and boards; they need to be helping negotiate service level agreements with providers and liaising with the police about local crime and safety issues. And they need to be acting as a neighbourhood champion within the local authority's decision-making and scrutiny forums.

The Local Government White Paper (2006) envisages local councillors having control of small local budgets and championing neighbourhoods through their key role in community calls for action. There are also to be more incentives and training to reduce the barriers facing people wanting to become elected members.

The importance of cultural change

Successful neighbourhood management means moving from paternalistic, centrally controlled service delivery, where outputs are relatively easy to predict and measure, to a more outcomes-based approach, sharing resources and power with others, including local communities, and taking more risks. This approach does not always sit comfortably with central government targets and auditing requirements, one of the many contradictions inherent in the neighbourhood agenda.

Although significant progress has been made, many organisations, including some housing providers, still have a long way to go. Organisational change is always challenging, but cultural change is particularly difficult. It requires people to change the way they think, not just the way they work, and is important on many levels – in the neighbourhood, in the service provider's organisation, in local partnership arrangements, in regional or sub-regional agencies and groupings and in central government.

Cultural change does not happen overnight; it takes time, and progress at one level is not always matched by progress at another, creating blockages and frustrations. There is always a temptation to cut corners, take the easier route and deliver less than anticipated or needed.

There is also a tendency for some organisations to think that a merger, a change of name, an internal reorganisation of systems and procedures and some staff training will do the trick. It won't. As many housing providers and others have found, there is a lot more to it than that. Neighbourhood management is an activity that demands a rigorous re-think of how organisations do things, what they deliver and why, and what sort of people they need to make it happen on the ground.

CULTURAL CHANGE: MAKING IT HAPPEN

Successful neighbourhood management requires organisations which:

- Have strong leadership
- Are fully committed to partnership or joined-up working at every level
- Employ staff with new skills and professional approaches
- Share knowledge, with clear communication up, down and across organisations
- Accept risk as part of change, and failure as part of learning, adopting new frameworks for performance measurement, regulation, audit and risk management
- Allow enough time for change
- Introduce procedures that join up accountability, information systems, action plans and outcomes effectively
- Have a community and neighbourhood-based approach to all aspects of their organisational structures, procedures and programmes.

Some service providers have found it easier to change their culture than others. In neighbourhood management terms the most startling change has been in the police service. There is much to learn from their experience.

A success story: neighbourhood policing

Over the past few years the police have been reinventing themselves. Once seen as remote, ineffective and bureaucratic by many communities desperate to see 'bobbies back on the beat' to tackle crime and anti-social behaviour, perceptions are now changing. Numbers of police and community support officers on the ground are increasing significantly, supplemented by neighbourhood and community wardens. The introduction of Crime and Disorder Reduction Partnerships, the government's *Together We Can* programme, the Respect agenda and neighbourhood policing all put a strong focus on police officers being much more in touch with local communities and their needs.

So how have they done it and what can other neighbourhood services – including housing providers – learn from their experience?

- **Resources** – neighbourhood policing has traditionally been under-resourced and not financially viable to operate on a long-term basis. This is now changing as central government funding increases and local forces unlock other resources from neighbourhood partners.

- **Boundaries** – police structures have been changed to work within neighbourhood boundaries. They have adapted their patches to fit; other service providers have found this difficult.

- **Improving performance and outcomes** – police experience in the neighbourhood management pathfinders suggests that both their short-term and long-term performance has improved, with a positive impact on crime rates in these neighbourhoods, over and above national trends. Interestingly, however, this is not necessarily linked to a reduction in the fear of crime among residents.

- **Experience** – the police ran a highly successful 3-year pilot programme (the national Reassurance Policing Programme) before committing to neighbourhood policing. They have seen the benefits, learned lessons and made the change.

- **Changing the image** – local policing was seen as a mundane activity by many potential recruits and certainly not a good career move. A lot of work has been done nationally and locally to turn this around, resulting in neighbourhood policing now being much more popular. Highly visible policing and a community-friendly style is also very popular with residents. Being visible, accessible, locally known and knowledgeable are all important for service providers.

- **Community engagement** – effective community engagement has been placed at the centre of the neighbourhood policing approach; working directly with communities pays off – it improves policing outcomes significantly.

- **Tackling community priorities first** – the success of neighbourhood police teams in neighbourhood management is not just about an increased presence on the streets and more consultation. It is also about new ways of gathering local information and working with other services to identify problems and agree long-term solutions. Putting community priorities first makes things happen more quickly, because most local residents want to help.

- **Co-location** – co-locating with other services at neighbourhood level has been a major plus, particularly where this has been done in neighbourhood or community hubs. It helps with information-sharing and coordination as well as improving the police image. In a number of places, the police have developed highly detailed local information, encouraging other service providers to follow suit.

Neighbourhood management: narrowing the gap

The key objective of the government's focus on neighbourhoods is to narrow the social and economic gap between the most deprived and the rest. Neighbourhood management was always expected to make an important contribution to this priority.

The pathfinder programme covers a wide variety of neighbourhoods, with very different levels of deprivation. Even so, all the pathfinders tend to score worse on many of the standard indices of deprivation than the local authorities in which they are based, although this does not mean that they are always the most deprived parts of these areas. This variation in deprivation levels is important for two reasons; it indicates that neighbourhood management is not an activity that should be restricted to deprived areas, but that narrowing the gap is an important objective, even in areas where deprivation is at a relatively low level.

Narrowing the health gap

GLOUCESTER COMMUNITY COUNTS NEIGHBOURHOOD MANAGEMENT PATHFINDER

Community Counts covers three neighbourhoods in Gloucester, where one-third of the population is from black and minority ethnic communities, mainly Asian and African-Caribbean. Health is a major theme for the pathfinder, with two key targets aiming to increase access to drug treatment by BME residents and reduce the number of those with diabetes requiring secondary health care. Narrowing the health gap is a top priority and some innovative approaches are being tried here.

The pathfinder found anecdotal evidence suggesting that despite relatively high usage in the BME community only a tiny percentage of people were accessing drug treatment in comparison to non-BME residents. A programme of awareness-raising has helped to reduce the stigma associated with drug misuse, particularly in the Muslim community, as well as providing advice to raise parental understanding and confidence.

Running in parallel, a locally-based, specialist GP took on the distribution of methadone and other treatments, reducing a six-month waiting list to two weeks. A community outreach team is targeting those still not accessing any treatments.

A specialist diabetes nurse has been funded though the neighbourhood management pathfinder, to change the way services are delivered and improve the ability of GP practices to deliver more targeted, culturally appropriate services.

A community peer educator scheme is providing accredited training to local volunteers, enabling them to work directly with BME communities, providing information about health issues in a variety of languages.

Tackling social exclusion in rural communities

TRANSFORM NORTH DEVON

Transform is a Round 2 neighbourhood management pathfinder focusing on three neighbourhoods in North Devon. Although these communities are in a rural setting, the issues they face are of an urban nature – poverty, low incomes, lack of recreational facilities, lack of access to services, poor housing conditions and lack of affordable housing.

The programme aims to improve quality of life and is tackling social exclusion in a number of ways, including local training opportunities, transport coordination and neighbourhood wardens.

The pathfinder has introduced a new way of training residents for an NVQ in catering and hospitality. Trainees have taken part in an intensive ten week on-the-job training course at a hotel in Ilfracombe. The scheme was run by North Devon College, with input from other training providers in the area. Eight of the nine trainees found employment at the end of the course.

A two year project is bringing together the buses run by a community transport association and a local car scheme under a single booking system managed by a new transport coordinator.

North Devon's first neighbourhood wardens have been taken on as 'Feet on the Street' in Ilfracombe, Combe Martin and Bratton Fleming. The pathfinder asked a group of residents in each community what they wanted wardens to do, and the consensus was that they should work with young people, look out for vulnerable people, bring old and young together, and be a point of contact between residents and agencies to help sort out any problems in the neighbourhood. Residents were keen that the wardens should not be seen as 'enforcers', but should be supporting youth activities, helping people to access services and breaking down barriers in the community.

So far, it is difficult to assess the pathfinders' progress on narrowing the gap. On certain deprivation indicators, some of the pathfinders have been making significant progress:

- In Knutton Cross Heath, Newcastle Under Lyme, from 2001/2 to 2004/5, the level of reported crime in the area fell by 17%, and fell faster than in the district as a whole, narrowing the gap from 33% higher crime than the district, to 11% higher.

- In Greater Hollington, Hastings, by 2004/5 there had been an 86% fall in the number of babies born to mothers who smoke, a 20% increase in levels of breastfeeding compared with only 9% in Hastings as a whole and a 15% reduction in teenage pregnancies.

Most of the measured improvements in all the pathfinders have been related to better coordination between service providers, more responsive and accessible services and improved perceptions among residents about these services. All these are important, but there is, as yet, no real evidence from the pathfinders that neighbourhood management is helping to 'narrow the gap', for example in educational attainment levels, health, mortality rates, youth unemployment or general worklessness. It is, perhaps, significant that employment and training agencies and some providers of youth services have been the least engaged in neighbourhood management initiatives so far.

Although it is certainly early days for many of the pathfinders, neighbourhood management has clearly performed better on tackling the more qualitative indices of deprivation – the 'clean, green, safe issues' – than on dealing with some of the more fundamental and entrenched drivers of deprivation, which inevitably take longer to turn around. This is unlikely to be changed by the new agenda for neighbourhoods, with its heavy emphasis on new forms of governance, community leadership and sanctions. Something more is needed.

Bringing together physical, social and economic renewal

The neighbourhood agenda is moving on. There is a real determination now to tackle neighbourhood deprivation in a much more comprehensive way. The physical (the development/renewal process), the economic (the potential to earn a livelihood and contribute to the wealth of the neighbourhood) and the social (enabling people to shape their neighbourhoods) are now recognised as fundamental and interrelated elements in creating successful communities. And tying together all three aspects is – or should be – the management of neighbourhoods: their governance and the provision of services. However, even some of the government's flagship programmes, despite their joined-up brief, have struggled to deliver all three aspects. Some of the New Deal for Communities programmes have been slow to develop neighbourhood management; many neighbourhood management pathfinders have been slow to attract investment in physical and economic renewal. The housing market renewal pathfinders have generally focused much more on balancing the housing market and physical change, than they have on creating successful neighbourhoods. As a result, many neighbourhoods have been changing for the better, but only in a piecemeal way.

The barrier between development and physical change in neighbourhoods on the one hand, and ongoing management and services on the other, is still a constraining force on delivering a truly joined-up neighbourhood programme. Many housing providers still suffer from this problem and they are not alone.

Physical, economic and social renewal

HATTERSLEY NEIGHBOURHOOD MANAGEMENT PATHFINDER, TAMESIDE

Hattersley is a large overspill estate on the outskirts of Manchester, built in the 1960s and 1970s to provide new rented homes for people affected by housing clearance in the east of the city. The estate was included as a Round 1 neighbourhood management pathfinder in 2002, but it was always recognised that Hattersley also needed significant investment in its physical infrastructure if its long-term future was to be secured.

The pathfinder has focused on three areas in its first years of operation:
- Improving the local environment, housing management and community safety
- Improving services for children and young people
- Supporting jobs and training.

Although much remains to be done, the outcomes so far have been impressive. Reported crime has fallen, educational attainment has risen, there is more demand for social housing, while resident satisfaction and external perceptions have both improved.

Plans for major physical redevelopment are now in place, linked to a stock transfer from Manchester City Council to a new local housing company, following a successful tenants' ballot in 2005.

The next 5-10 years will be an interesting time for the estate as the physical redevelopments start to take place. The continuation of neighbourhood management through this transitional phase will be crucial. There should be opportunities to mainstream the programme through financial contributions and other forms of support from the lead developer and housing associations, along with the key service providers.

Neighbourhood management, which encompasses so many elements, is the big challenge for the future. But what does it mean in practice, beyond tackling the basic liveability issues?

- In priority areas of substantial clearance and new development, neighbourhood management should be aimed at **managing transition**
- In areas of partial clearance and some new development, neighbourhood management should be aimed at **stabilising the community and managing transition**
- In areas of new development, neighbourhood management should be aimed at **developing new communities and integrating those adjacent**
- In areas of little physical change, neighbourhood management should be aimed at **service consolidation and improvement**
- In neighbourhoods with dedicated organisations focused on renewal and regeneration, exit strategies for these time-limited programmes should normally include their **evolution into a long-term neighbourhood management body**
- In all areas, neighbourhood management needs to place a new emphasis on **narrowing the economic and social gap**, through targeted programmes aimed at reducing worklessness and particularly youth unemployment, through greater engagement with jobs and training agencies and targeted programmes of support.

There is a role here for everyone involved in neighbourhood programmes, not just the public and voluntary sectors. Private housebuilders and developers can contribute through community investment, dowries and trust funds, to leave behind a sustainable infrastructure which will help neighbourhoods remain successful once they have gone.

Private sector support for neighbourhood management

CATERHAM URBAN VILLAGE, SURREY

Caterham Urban Village is a former Ministry of Defence barracks, declared surplus to requirements in 1990. With the site earmarked for housing redevelopment, local councillors were keen to ensure that many of the existing buildings were retained and that the scheme had a strong community component.

Working with the appointed developer, Linden Homes, the local authority decided to develop plans for an urban village, providing a viable balance of employment opportunities, community facilities and new homes.

Community representatives set up a trust to make sure that their views were central to the urban village plans. It negotiated with the developer and the local authority to secure a substantial community dowry, through the use of Section 106 agreements.

→

Linden Homes contributed over £2 million, helping to finance a range of social and community projects, including a restored cricket ground, chapel, and two gyms. The community trust has also used some of this money to fund a neighbourhood management approach to asset management.

This was a difficult project for the private sector, not least because conservation area status imposed limitations on what could be done with some of the buildings. However, the creation of the community trust and their ability to take on some of these buildings enabled Linden Homes to build the site on a profitable basis.

Setting new standards for service providers

To achieve real change, neighbourhood management must secure reliable, high quality and cost effective services which meet local communities' needs and expectations. Where this proves difficult, sanctions will be needed to improve performance and provide redress. Encouragement is unlikely to be enough, something which has been recognised by the 2006 Local Government White Paper. Neighbourhood management needs to be given some teeth.

This crucial step cannot be fudged through the use of more reporting mechanisms, service level agreements, performance management frameworks and joined-up targets – useful as these are. The impact of neighbourhood management, as it moves into the mainstream, will be much greater if all neighbourhood service providers are required to work to a set of locally agreed standards, and communities have the power to invoke sanctions against those that under-perform. Sanctions for under-performance are nothing new. Some neighbourhood management initiatives have been using carrots and sticks successfully for many years, for example, through neighbourhood agreements.

Neighbourhood standards are as much about approach and attitudes as setting and meeting targets. Changing attitudes is, however, not a one-way street. Communities need to become more active in 'self-policing' their neighbourhoods, and taking more control over the local environment; many already do. There is, however, a danger that the neighbourhood agenda will reinforce the notion that everything is the responsibility of someone else, when the reality is that a joint effort is needed by everyone to maintain decent neighbourhood standards. Making sure service delivery standards are agreed between providers and communities is key, but these agreements also have to be enforceable.

However, communities will not be able to use service enforcement powers effectively unless they understand their rights and have sufficient strength to initiate actions and follow them through in a structured and credible way. Building the strength of local communities – a vital aspect of the whole new agenda for neighbourhoods – is covered in detail in the next chapter.

Sharing responsbility for changing neighbourhoods
SPRINGBOURNE AND BOSCOMBE WEST, BOURNEMOUTH

Springbourne and Boscombe West in Bournemouth is fairly typical of many low income, older private sector neighbourhoods. There is significant homelessness locally and many of those affected end up living in sub-standard private rented properties, many in multiple occupation.

As a direct response to this issue the neighbourhood management pathfinder set up a Landlord Licensing and Tenant Accreditation Scheme. To complement it, innovative one-off projects have encouraged tenants and owner occupiers to come together to enjoy themselves and collectively make improvements to the outside of their properties.

It has been difficult to engage with private landlords, who have been slow to change their practices, despite pressure from the local community. The pathfinder helped, by pressing the local authority to take action against some of them under Section 215 of the Town and Planning Act 1990, demonstrating the need to use enforcement where appropriate to change attitudes, change the way services are provided, and respond positively to community concerns.

Developing a sense of community is always important, particularly in neighbourhoods where some people move on quickly and stability is difficult to achieve. The shared responsibility for delivering change has also led to the establishment of a 'Home Watch Group'. Residents have raised money for the local park, and this has encouraged the police to tackle anti-social behaviour there.

Strengthening the housing provider's role

Affordable housing providers can be found everywhere in deprived neighbourhoods and increasingly in those that are not deprived. In many of these places they are now the major asset holder. They have a vested interest in making sure these neighbourhoods are well managed. A huge shift in thinking and doing is required for housing providers to move from managing their housing stock to managing places. Much of this is still in its infancy, although there are some useful examples of good practice, such as those providers involved in the Investors in Communities programme – a recognition scheme for residents, housing associations and local authorities working together to build safe and stable communities.

Despite great strides made by some providers, neighbourhood management is still seen by most as an increasingly important activity, but one which is not yet a mainstream priority. While there is growing evidence of housing provider engagement in low-level 'housing plus' type activities, there are still not enough examples of them leading the process of neighbourhood management, or even supporting individual components of it.

Housing providers leading neighbourhood management
TOUCHSTONE HOUSING ASSOCIATION, WOLVERHAMPTON

Wolverhampton City Council has piloted neighbourhood management in seven 'natural neighbourhoods' across the City. Each pilot is led by a different managing agent. Touchstone Housing was the accountable body and managing agent for over three years for the pilot in the ethnically mixed Whitmore Reans and Dunstall area and was the first housing association in the country to lead a neighbourhood management initiative.

Touchstone got involved in the pilot as the majority landlord; neighbourhood management clearly fitted with its overall corporate vision of 'building better places to live' through investing in homes, communities and individuals. It has used the pilot to look more strategically at the way it develops and delivers its core business in the city as a whole. The pilot has enabled it to experiment with combining neighbourhood management with its Local Management Plan to meet financial, service and social objectives.

The pilot has made a major contribution to making the neighbourhood a more popular and more attractive place to live and has allowed it to develop new ways of working with local residents to challenge the inequalities and problems that they experience.

Abstracted from *Up Your Street: Housing associations and the neighbourhoods and communities agenda* (Housing Corporation 2006).

There is a notable regional difference in housing provider led activity in neighbourhood management, with significant involvement in north west England, but rather less elsewhere. Some of the best examples of housing-led neighbourhood management are to be found among geographically-focused housing organisations – community-based housing associations, tenant management organisations and local housing companies. But much good work is also being done by larger, national and regional associations, including some of the large-scale voluntary transfer associations. Arms length management organisations (ALMOs) have yet to make a significant national contribution however – possibly due to their focus on meeting the government's Decent Homes Standard.

Meanwhile, many housing providers are playing a useful role on neighbourhood management partnership boards and through active partnerships with other service providers. They are involved in 12 of the 15 Round 2 pathfinders. Where they have led, housing providers have taken an holistic view of neighbourhoods, pulling together a wide range of service providers to deliver change for local communities. Where they have been in a supportive role, housing providers have acted as managing agents, co-ordinated landlords' input and influenced major change in housing governance, through the creation of ALMOs and stock transfers. They have tended to be more cautious about stepping too far outside their core business activity.

In embarking on neighbourhood management, housing providers should be clear about their reasons for getting involved and about the need for adopting new skills and significant cultural change. Chapter 7 looks in detail at how housing providers should respond to the neighbourhood agenda. The next chapter focuses on the central role of local communities.

NEIGHBOURHOOD MANAGEMENT

WHAT HOUSING PROVIDERS CAN DO TO MAKE IT HAPPEN

- Initiate discussions with local authorities, community organisations and other service providers about establishing neighbourhood management in areas of significant stock-holding; don't wait for others to take a lead
- Work through LSPs and LAAs to secure funding and support for neighbourhood management roll out into priority neighbourhoods
- Look for innovative ways of funding neighbourhood management activities, including gifting land, sale and lease-back deals and equity sharing arrangements to generate long-term revenue
- Provide internal resources (staff, office space and facilities and training) for neighbourhood management activity – particularly community engagement

→

- Sponsor community planning exercises and opinion surveys among residents, to gauge the interest in neighbourhood management, and then respond accordingly
- Broker negotiations with other housing providers in the same neighbourhood about the potential for rationalising management or stock
- Facilitate the setting up of small neighbourhood-based, community-run service bodies, such as environmental clean-up squads and neighbourhood wardens
- Assess the potential for the transfer of management responsibilities for the neighbourhood's social housing stock to a community-run body.

CHAPTER 6

LOCAL COMMUNITIES: IN THE DRIVING SEAT?

This chapter is about how to put devolution into practice at neighbourhood level. It stresses the importance of raising the profile of community engagement in the neighbourhood agenda. It looks at how housing can be the focus for strengthening communities and at how some communities have already taken a lead role in transforming their own neighbourhoods.

The neighbourhood agenda aims to empower communities in all neighbourhoods, but especially in deprived areas. There has been a step change in the level of interest and a steady growth in the number of good practice examples up and down the country. However, there remain significant challenges in making it happen across the board and real dangers that it won't happen unless the right conditions are put in place.

Creating real opportunities, building capacity, removing barriers, offering active encouragement and support, and providing the means to apply sanctions are all pre-requisites for success, but they will not, in themselves, produce genuinely empowered neighbourhoods. Something more fundamental is required.

The real issues here are about power and money – the mechanisms, sanctions, rights and responsibilities to wield power and the resources to back it up. There is no real control without both, whether in neighbourhoods or any other aspect of life. One of the concerns about the devolution agenda is that the renewed faith in local government's ability to deliver national priorities at local level will not be accompanied by a similar willingness by local authorities and others to transfer power and responsibility to the neighbourhood.

Putting communities in the driving seat also requires a fundamental cultural shift in organisations. Cultures have begun to change in this respect in many places, but success requires visionary, determined leadership backed by enthusiastic, committed staff. Without these, there is the danger that alongside new rhetoric and responsibilities, many of the individuals and their old ways of working still remain.

Much the same can be said of many communities themselves. The dependency culture is still embedded on many (though by no means all) estates; most people expect 'the council' to do everything and while more than happy to criticise them when they don't, they tend to leave doing something about it to others. 'The others' are often a small group of committed, but over-stretched and under-valued volunteers.

Changing the balance of power presents many challenges, but it is not an unachievable goal and, crucially, it remains the key to making neighbourhoods successful.

Community engagement: making it happen

Engaging with local communities is now current practice among most housing providers and, indeed, most agencies providing services to the public. Although attitudes are changing, for some neighbourhood service providers, community engagement still seems to be more of a time-consuming chore that needs to be done, rather than an approach that brings its own benefits and leads to lasting change.

Among other things, successful community engagement:
- Builds sustainable communities and successful neighbourhoods
- Promotes social inclusion
- Challenges discrimination
- Strengthens community cohesion
- Empowers ordinary people
- Improves public service standards and local delivery
- Makes regeneration investment sustainable in the long term.

A successful community engagement approach in neighbourhoods might usefully include:
- Getting local people involved right from the start
- Using 'what works' methods of disseminating information – these will be different in each community
- Prioritising informal and participative methods of consultation – avoiding formal public meetings
- Identifying and targeting rarely-heard groups, particularly those that do not normally get involved in community activities

- Working with and building on existing structures where these are appropriate
- Helping to put new structures in place where no suitable neighbourhood ones exist
- Recruiting local people into these new structures and encouraging 'ownership' of the process
- Encouraging flexibility, so that these structures can evolve as residents gain in confidence and experience
- Developing residents' leadership skills
- Promoting and sustaining democratic neighbourhood representation through annual elections
- Running an extensive community consultation process using well-established techniques (community planning, 'planning for real', citizens' juries, ballots)
- Developing neighbourhood or community plans which outline residents' agendas for change
- Providing community development and, when needed, independent advice
- Creating a culture of trust, transparency and accountability, with no hidden agendas
- Treating residents as equals and working with them on this basis
- Training and supporting community representatives involved in neighbourhood issues
- Providing community access to resources to pursue their own objectives
- Moving at the community's pace, allowing adequate time for consultation and involvement to be effective
- Being process and outcome-led rather than funding-led (not always easy)
- Focusing on good communications, providing maximum rather than minimum information to residents.

Engaging communities in developing a community housing plan
HARTLEPOOL NEW DEAL FOR COMMUNITIES

Faced with a slump in the local housing market and abandonment of some terrace properties in central Hartlepool, this New Deal for Communities programme prioritised housing intervention within its delivery plan and in 2002, with the full support of the local authority, began work on a Community Housing Plan. It proved to be one of the most intensive resident-led processes ever undertaken in a neighbourhood, involving more than 1,500 residents.

→

Led by external consultants SRC, the community housing plan process involved:

- An initial 6 month community strengthening programme, followed by a 15 month plan development period, working at the residents' pace

- 65 street and neighbourhood workshops to fully engage residents in the plan-making process

- An outreach programme, with specific workshops and informal sessions with hard-to-reach groups, feeding their views into the plan-making process

- The use of interactive, hands-on modelling and virtual reality techniques to show residents different ways of changing terraces, streets and neighbourhoods

- Street-by-street resident ballots on the options for physical change, including selective demolition, involving one-third of the area's 4,500 households

- The recruitment and training of local residents as a local support team, employed by NDC, but managed by the external consultants

- Setting up a community-led Housing Regeneration Company, in partnership with a local housing association and the council, to deliver the Plan

- Regular progress reports to community representatives and a highly accessible, plain English Community Housing Plan document at the end.

The Community Housing Plan is now being delivered. It is rare for owner-occupiers to vote for the demolition of their own homes, but that is what happened here – a testament to both the strength of the community engagement process and perhaps the emphasis on a good financial compensation package.

Community development

Community development is the starting point for achieving sustainable change in neighbourhoods and needs to be adequately resourced. While the number of community development workers employed by local authority departments has dwindled in recent years, many housing providers have responded by establishing community development teams; other agencies involved in neighbourhoods have done the same. They have helped to provide a clear mechanism through which local communities can engage with agencies traditionally seen as remote and inaccessible.

Strengthening the ability of local groups to build their structures, systems, people and skills is an essential part of a broader community development approach.

THE 7 Es OF COMMUNITY DEVELOPMENT

1. **Enabling** people to become involved by removing practical barriers to their participation

2. **Encouraging** individuals to contribute to activities and decision-making

3. **Empowering** others by increasing their confidence and ability to influence decisions and take responsibility

4. **Educating** people by helping them to reflect on their own experience

5. **Equalising** situations so that people have the same access to opportunities, resources and facilities

6. **Evaluating** the impact of these interventions

7. **Engaging** with groups and organisations to increase community involvement in public decision-making.

Abstracted from Gilchrist, A (2004) *The Well-Connected Community: A networking approach to community development*, The Community Development Foundation.

Community development as part of the core business

RHONDDA HOUSING ASSOCIATION, SOUTH WALES

Rhondda Housing Association is a small/medium sized housing association, operating in south Wales. It owns and manages 1,500 homes in an area with the highest levels of deprivation in the country. The association began engaging with the community development agenda eight years ago and since then it has been regarded as part of their core business, now linked closely to neighbourhood management initiatives. Committee members and staff now see community development as equal in importance to collecting the rents and maintaining their homes.

This means that alongside its neighbourhood-based housing management work the association has involved itself in a rich variety of 'quality of life' initiatives for a wide range of age groups, including:

- Youth engagement and advocacy projects
- Construction skills training through the Young Builders Trust
- Community health development, healthy living advice and a food cooperative
- Parental support classes and after-school clubs

→

- Environmental action
- Time exchange schemes
- Village forums.

The association has accessed many different funding streams to carry out this work and has itself become a community resource. It has a core staff of seven people, with another eight employed on behalf of community groups in the area.

Strengthening communities

Many professionals are likely to assume that residents require intensive training before they can be expected to participate in decisions about their neighbourhoods. This is not always so – most people learn best 'on the job' and formal training sessions, however well delivered, can put people off. Ideally, the need for training and learning should come from doing, and be identified by people themselves. There is a big difference between training and strengthening (or capacity building); the former invariably equips people to work in the way that agencies traditionally work; the latter develops people's personal abilities, such as confidence, self-esteem and understanding. Both are important. CIH with support from the Academy for Sustainable Communities (ASC) is developing an *Active Learning for Residents* framework which will recognise the skills, knowledge and competence which tenants and residents acquire through active involvement in their local communities.

Strengthening communities is a high-risk activity; the outcomes are never known in advance; in deprived neighbourhoods, the local people involved are almost always under pressure, personally, socially and economically. Community representatives are volunteers – many of them are involved in a wide range of activities and local organisations. They are exposed to the everyday pressures of life in deprived neighbourhoods; many suffer from poor health, which may be compounded by the stress and long hours they put in.

Perhaps not surprisingly, 'consultation fatigue' is an increasing concern, particularly where communities have been consulted several times with no obvious action following on. As community involvement in the neighbourhood agenda becomes ever more important, so this particular issue is likely to be more widely understood.

Agencies working with local communities in neighbourhoods should therefore:

- Appreciate that residents do not get paid for being involved and need to see positive and early results of their efforts

- Work within the capacity of individuals
- Develop people's confidence, self-esteem and understanding
- Plan for a potential turnover of key individuals
- Examine ways of offering volunteers rewards for their work if appropriate
- Support independent, community-led organisations as a vital building block for effective engagement
- Broaden the base of people involved in community activity, to enable workloads to be shared
- Ensure that those involved have real influence.

Strengthening communities through participation
MANTON COMMUNITY ALLIANCE, BASSETLAW

Manton Community Alliance is a Round 2 neighbourhood management pathfinder. It has developed a 'behaviour-not-project' model approach towards neighbourhood renewal, which is changing the relationship between residents and service providers and giving a boost to participatory democracy.

In Manton, community engagement is driven by residents and coordinated by the pathfinder on behalf of all the public services working in the neighbourhood. A formal agreement has been signed with the local ALMO, which gives the resident-led pathfinder the lead role on community engagement.

The main outcomes have so far been impressive:

- The culture and behaviour of local service providers is beginning to change, with associated improvements in service delivery
- There is an increased mutual understanding between residents and providers, with associated improved satisfaction levels, better quality information and a reduced 'expectation gap'
- Engagement between local elected representatives and the local community, through the Partnership, has improved significantly
- A growing number of residents are taking on community leadership positions – eg as ALMO board members and school governors.

The Partnership is now negotiating a neighbourhood charter and plans to develop a staged approach to participatory budgeting.

Building capacity among young people

OLDINGTON AND FOLEY PARK, KIDDERMINSTER NEIGHBOURHOOD MANAGEMENT PATHFINDER

The Oldington and Foley Park Pathfinder works with children and young people on a Junior Pathfinders programme, in an area with low levels of educational achievement. The Junior Pathfinders developed their own young people's charter, *Small People with Big Ideas*, written entirely in their own words.

The Junior Pathfinders began when the neighbourhood management staff organised a fun day at the school and the pupils reported after the event that they could do it better, and they did! Now the young people organise fun days, award ceremonies, team events, outward bound holidays and healthy eating days. They have also made presentations at several national conferences.

The Junior Pathfinders have their own Community Chest which carries a high level of responsibility. Last year a group of Junior Reporters interviewed their local MP and others about the neighbourhood management work in the area, with the completed interviews broadcast on the local BBC news.

The school now not only hosts the neighbourhood management team, but also a local base for the police and Sure Start, and plans are being developed to include space for a community health service, adult learning and for local housing association staff.

Strengthening local communities requires resources and dedicated, experienced staff. It can also be a process which leads directly to the creation of local jobs, providing support for fragile local economies. New neighbourhood services can be provided by residents themselves, while existing ones can target local people for recruitment. Some housing providers have a long history of generating local employment through their community investment activities. Much of this has, in the past, been focused around construction and development, but the new agenda for neighbourhoods opens up broader opportunities for service jobs of a less transitory nature.

Engaging with black and minority ethnic communities

Taking concerted action to consult with and involve black and minority ethnic communities in neighbourhoods has assumed growing importance in recent years. On most measures of social exclusion, BME communities are faring worse than white communities, nowhere more so than in the deprived neighbourhoods. Many BME communities themselves have become much more assertive in recent years, but few would describe themselves as being in the driving seat.

The political emphasis placed on community cohesion and the greater emphasis given to community engagement generally have both meant that organisations working in neighbourhoods are more aware of black and minority ethnic issues and have learned how to work more appropriately with them. However, there is still an overwhelmingly white culture in the great majority of housing providers and indeed most agencies working in neighbourhoods. There is also a continuing gap between the seemingly widespread acceptance of the need to take measures to consult with and involve BME communities, and actually doing it. There is suspicion and lack of trust between many BME communities and neighbourhood service providers, a problem that has been exacerbated by the high-profile national events of recent years. In many areas there is also now a need for neighbourhood agencies to engage with new migrants from the EU accession states.

The experience of those housing providers and others who have engaged successfully with BME communities suggests that the principles for consulting with and involving BME communities are broadly the same as those for any community:

- Tapping into their (not always overtly expressed) desire to be actively involved, instead of treating them as passive recipients
- Understanding that they may want to be involved at every level, including management and delivery
- Ensuring that engagement leads to action which reflects the views and needs expressed
- Ensuring they are involved on a proportionate basis, that they get the appropriate amount of consultation time and effort in relation to the size and nature of the community
- Understanding that consultation about how to engage may be necessary
- Appreciating that there is likely to be suspicion, and cynicism born of previous inadequate consultation or lack of action
- Recognising sub-groups, such as young people, women, older people and refugees and asylum seekers.

In addition, there are three specific principles:

- Ensuring that a range of methods and structures are applied which are sensitive to the varying traditions and cultures of the wide range of communities under the BME umbrella
- Appreciating that, for a variety of reasons, many BME communities have only a relatively recent history of consultation and involvement, on an individual or community level
- Recognising that for BME communities neighbourhood decline is not just about poverty, but may also be about racial discrimination.

Most BME communities have real strengths which can help with the engagement process. These include:

- Strong networks in areas, and across tenures, which can relay information very quickly and effectively
- Strong cultural identities, which can focus activity, for example around celebrations and events
- Strong faith identities, which can focus activity, such as those around places of worship.

Practical suggestions for engaging effectively with BME communities include the following:

- Conduct a survey of BME residents or analysis of all survey results by ethnicity
- Hold focus groups or community conferences that target different BME or faith groups
- Support and get involved in community celebrations
- Help to establish and support BME residents' groups
- Provide training and support for residents' groups to achieve equality goals
- Consult BME housing associations and other organisations on how best to involve BME communities
- Provide capacity building and support for community groups
- Set action plans with targets for the take-up of employment opportunities and other outputs of regeneration programmes.

Engaging with Islamic communities

ASHRAM HOUSING ASSOCIATION

Ashram Housing Association owns and manages 1,000 homes in a small number of tightly-defined neighbourhoods in the West Midlands. The association works with deprived, mainly Islamic communities and has developed a highly varied and successful programme of engagement with them.

Many Islamic women have traditionally found it difficult to engage in local housing issues, something Ashram was determined to tackle. They established the Regional BME Women's Housing Network so that local women were aware of emerging issues and could get involved in the debate, and many have done so. The Network feeds into the formal regional housing process.

→

In partnership with the University of Central England, Ashram is running a series of community design workshops for women, to introduce local women to design concepts, basic principles of urban design and to investigate a new typology of building influenced by South Asian cultures.

As part of the association's financial inclusion strategy the association is providing advice and assistance to an enterprising food co-operative run by local Bangladeshi women and is also involved in a number of other credit and savings initiatives.

'Ashram Angels' who progressed through to the national BBC 5-a-side competition, are playing their part in breaking down another sporting taboo by encouraging Asian women to take up football as a means of improving health and self confidence.

Ashram also has a project *Every Child Matters, But It Takes A Village*, which involves a range of joint initiatives with local schools including student placements, curriculum support, mentoring programmes and the production of careers DVDs. In 2006 the partnership won the Education Business Partnership for Industry award.

Engaging with refugees and asylum seekers

Most BME communities have long-established roots in their neighbourhoods; asylum seekers and refugees do not. Engaging successfully with them is often difficult and needs to be carefully handled. The immediate concerns of established residents and newcomers differ in many neighbourhoods; established residents are often worried about competition for scarce resources, while safety and security are usually top of most newcomers' priorities.

Cultural and language difficulties contribute to misunderstanding, rumour and myth, and more preparatory work needs to be done in neighbourhoods to prepare established residents for the arrival of newcomers. Attitudes often change, however, when people get together and begin to understand each others' fears and aspirations. Setting up mutually-beneficial projects is one way of bridging the gap and there are many examples of good practice up and down the country. A good example is the Refugee Accommodate Project run by Canopy Housing in Leeds, where volunteers from local host and asylum-seeking communities work together to refurbish derelict and disused houses to provide homes for refugees and homeless locals alike.

Community-based drama

HACT'S COMMUNITIES R US PROJECT IN BOLTON

Hact (Housing Associations Charitable Trust) has a project – Communities R Us – which is promoting contact at neighbourhood level between different communities, focusing particularly on three areas where there has been recent migration. One of these, supported by Bolton Community Homes, is in the Derby Road/Deane Road area of Bolton where the long-term residents including Asians have seen a lot of change recently with the arrival of a number of new refugee residents – including Somalis, Iraqi Kurds, Francophone and other Africans.

One aspect of the project has been a community-based drama. The drama provided the catalyst for discussion, which may help to realise aspirations and resolve problems within the area. Painstaking door-to-door consultation provided material for the drama, with actors recruited from the neighbourhood, to 'play back' opinions about the area in a way which provoked discussion and helped to demonstrate that concerns are shared. The drama was organised by a local person with experience in this field.

The drama consisted of eight sketches. The actors were Somali, Indian Hindu, Muslim Asian and Kurdish. The sketches mainly relied on mime to be understood, and they were watched by over 100 people of all ages. The audience clearly found it thought provoking and interesting. They were given opportunities to comment, for example post-it notes were distributed before the performance and a workshop discussion held immediately afterwards. The discussion led to several positive comments about improving the area and to some active discussions between members of the three main resident groups (white, Asian and refugees). A follow-up meeting has decided that it is a priority to hold more shared events dealing with neighbourhood issues.

Engaging with rural communities

Delivering successful neighbourhoods in rural areas and involving local communities in the process pose different problems to those in urban areas. Rural communities have particular issues that make the neighbourhood agenda more difficult to deliver. While many of the techniques and processes involved in managing rural neighbourhoods are little different from those needed in urban areas, there are additional challenges, including:

- Communities are smaller and more dispersed
- Communities of interest often rank alongside communities of geography

- Housing providers rarely have large stock holdings in individual neighbourhoods, villages or towns and lack the critical mass to have the resources to make a significant impact on neighbourhood problems
- Many of the funding sources available for community initiatives in urban areas are not available in rural areas
- Community development workers and capacity building staff are spread very thinly
- Resident and tenant involvement is under-developed in rural areas, compared with their urban counterparts
- The loss of important community facilities, such as village shops, post offices and public transport, which often underpin community life in isolated areas
- The absence of a community centre or meeting place, which adds to people's feeling of social isolation
- Rural poverty and a lack of job opportunities, particularly in areas where old industries have closed down.

However, despite these substantial difficulties, there is growing interest among policy-makers in tackling rural deprivation and a greater recognition that this is an increasingly important issue. None of these problems is insuperable. Small, isolated communities are getting together through a number of rural initiatives.

Developing community assets

HARRISTON VILLAGE HALL, WEST CUMBRIA

Harriston is a rare example of a housing association supporting the development of a rural village hall. It shows what can be done by housing providers working with local communities and with very limited resources.

Derwent and Solway Housing Association has been supporting the development of a village hall trust in Harriston, an ex-mining village in West Cumbria. The housing association owns almost all of the 98 properties in Harriston following a borough-wide stock transfer in 1999.

The village hall is a former mission chapel and is being leased to Harriston Community Centre Group for a peppercorn rent from the housing association. The community group is being supported by the association's Neighbourhood Regeneration Officer.

→

Although there are no other community facilities in the village, it has a great community spirit. The village hall is run entirely by volunteers, with a full programme of activities for all ages thoughout the week and every weekend, including a drop-in facility for young people. There is a new partnership with Age Concern and much-needed decorating is being carried out with the workforce from the Probation Service's Community Payback Scheme.

Voluntary Action Cumbria are also supporting the group to become a registered charity, opening up more opportunities for attracting funding for new activities and essential structural building work.

Community Land Trusts (CLTs) are a relatively new mechanism for achieving democratic ownership of land by the local community and the management of local assets, similar to Development Trusts (see chapter 3). Although by no means exclusive to rural neighbourhoods, they do have perhaps their greatest potential here. Land is taken out of the market and separated from its productive use so that the impact of land appreciation is removed, enabling long-term affordable and sustainable local development. Through CLTs, local residents and businesses participate in, and take responsibility for, planning and delivering redevelopment schemes.

CLT activities include:

- Developing affordable housing to rent or buy for members of the community
- Enabling residents on lower incomes to acquire an economic interest in the success of their community
- Developing land for affordable workspace and retail units
- Providing and maintaining community facilities for social and public services
- Managing green spaces, conservation areas and providing access for new entrants to farming
- Promoting resident involvement, local democracy and active citizenship.

Securing community benefit from rising land values
STONESFIELD COMMUNITY LAND TRUST, OXFORDSHIRE

In the early 1980s, steep rises in land value in West Oxfordshire had a destructive effect on many village communities. In response, Stonesfield Community Trust (SCT) was founded in 1983. Local activist Tony Crofts donated a quarter-acre site in the village of Stonesfield for affordable housing for local people in perpetuity.

→

A seedcorn grant of £3,000 from a local company was used to register the Trust and negotiate planning permission, which alone increased the value of the donated land from £3,500 to £150,000, enabling SCT to raise a mortgage and build the first six homes. SCT has since borrowed additional funds from the local authority and ethical investors.

The Trust has developed a further five affordable homes on another quarter-acre site, and converted a redundant glove factory into a base for the village pre-school. More recently, a second development has been completed to provide three more homes and house the village post office at a low fixed rent. All properties have high energy efficiency standards to ensure low running costs. In 2005 the first loans were fully repaid and net income from CLT property will soon fund a local youth service. In a few years time, the net income generated by CLT rents for community purposes in the village will be £40,000 a year.

How involved are local communities in their neighbourhoods?

The new agenda for neighbourhoods pre-supposes that there are large numbers of un-engaged residents waiting to play a more active role in their community. This is some way from reality in most places. Most neighbourhoods have a core group of people who are involved in community activity, usually as volunteers, but some are always more active than others.

Many tenants' and residents' associations find that, although their membership lists may be quite healthy, attendance at regular meetings is often low, swelling dramatically only when a 'hot issue' emerges. Similarly, LSVT ballots usually attract a high turnout of voters. Keeping large numbers of residents actively engaged in ongoing programmes, like neighbourhood management and community associations managing local assets, is always more of a challenge. Most community groups have dealt with this by bolting on a wide range of social activities to their core business.

Residents get involved in their neighbourhoods for different reasons; their attitudes vary too – from the activity motivated 'can-do'ers' to the 'wait and see'ers' who want to see which way the wind blows before committing themselves. Professionals have a range of different attitudes too, and one of the problems of working in neighbourhoods is that there is often an ongoing mismatch between the attitudes of residents and those of professionals. Matching the right people to the right job is critically important for achieving positive outcomes.

Although the *quantity* of residents involved in neighbourhood activities may be smaller than might be expected, it is the *quality* of engagement that is arguably more important.

People are usually more interested in specific, local matters rather than the wider, more strategic issues. Where major change is planned, key factors affecting the proportion of residents likely to be involved include the size of the area under consideration and the length of the delivery timeframe:

- For example, in some of the housing market renewal areas in northern England, 10-20% of residents have been actively involved in helping draw up strategic visions and area development frameworks where 10,000-20,000 homes were involved.

- By contrast, in some of the smaller housing market renewal areas in north east England, for example, between 30% and 40% of residents have been actively involved in developing neighbourhood action plans for 500-5,000 homes.

A high quality community engagement process

MANNINGHAM NEIGHBOURHOOD MASTERPLAN, BRADFORD

Manningham is a large, complex, multi-cultural neighbourhood where many residents are reluctant to engage, while others feel over-consulted. There is a widespread lack of understanding of how the place actually works, and this makes it difficult to deliver positive change. Community engagement needs careful planning to reflect these circumstances.

Carried out in 2004-2005, the Manningham masterplan involved a 6 month intensive piece of in-depth qualitative community engagement, aimed at finding out how people live, how they interact with each other and how they see their future.

The process involved talking to a large cross section of ordinary residents, young and old, religious leaders, shopkeepers, locally-based agencies and business people. Consultants SRC talked to them individually, at meetings, on the doorstep, and in groups walking round the streets. People were interviewed formally, informally and were asked to role-play at story-telling sessions.

There were 'drop-ins' at community venues across Manningham, women-only and young people's sessions, a sample Community Attitudes survey carried out on the doorstep and workshops for local business leaders. People responded very positively to what must have seemed to most of them yet another round of consultation with little prospect of action at the end of it.

→

Much of the consultation period coincided with the Muslim holy month of Ramadan, which restricted engagement with large numbers of people. With a different timescale, sessions would have been held through the Imams after Friday prayers and additional weekend or evening events in community centres.

Despite these limitations, more than 500 local residents were involved in drawing up the masterplan. But more importantly, the final masterplan was informed by a much better understanding of Manningham's many communities, their needs and aspirations.

It is worth remembering that people have a right not to be involved and that non-involvement is not always due to apathy. People must always be given the opportunity to engage in improving their neighbourhood and in a way which enables them to do so easily, even though the majority will probably not do so; in reality most people are 'wait and see'ers' and just want to get on with their lives. But in some neighbourhoods, this conventional wisdom has been turned on its head.

Taking more control

For a growing number of communities, being asked for their views and being offered involvement in making decisions about their neighbourhoods does not go far enough. Some of the partnerships that communities are being encouraged to join can feel too bureaucratic; others may be dominated by professionals or local politicians. Consultation can sometimes seem to be never-ending, even delaying much-needed action.

For these communities, taking control of some of the things that happen or need to happen in their neighbourhood can make good sense. But it is not easy; those who have done it have usually found it to be a long, hard, if ultimately rewarding road.

Communities that have some control over what happens in their neighbourhood can:

- Bring local people together and help create a sense of identity which may have been absent before; it can focus people's minds, as well as their efforts, on tackling issues collectively
- Encourage people to develop a sense of local pride, community spirit and togetherness that may have been absent for many years
- Offer new opportunities for the non-joiners in local communities to get involved and feel included, rather than excluded

- Make sure local services really do meet community needs, by relying less on outside bodies
- Empower individuals, enabling them to use skills they never knew they had, or develop new ones
- Produce a great feeling of satisfaction in people who are doing things for themselves and achieving things, perhaps for the first time
- Create some much-needed local jobs.

But it is not all plain sailing:

- It means taking on responsibility and liability
- It usually needs a lot of voluntary effort
- It always seems to take longer to achieve things than people expect
- It is never easy to get enough people actively involved to share responsibility for all the tasks that need to be done
- There is bound to be some opposition; developing a thick skin is a definite advantage
- It is not always easy to find the right sort of help needed to get going
- It can be difficult to get hold of money or other resources
- It might not work. Some community-controlled initiatives fail, for all sorts of reasons.

Community pressure delivers a neighbourhood hub
BENTILEE DISTRICT CENTRE, STOKE-ON-TRENT

Driven from day one by the local community, the pioneering Bentilee District Centre is a good example of joined-up neighbourhood service delivery, providing a wide range of local services all under one roof. Bentilee District Centre has become a reality against all the odds because of the determination of a core group of local residents who have captured the support of the wider community.

The Bentilee District Centre PFI project is a £50 million CLG national pathfinder scheme; built in a deprived housing estate in inner city Stoke, its aim is to transform the quality of life of the people of Bentilee.

The Centre has been driven entirely by a small group of local people who were not prepared to accept the raw deal they felt their community was getting from the public and private sectors. They managed to rally the support of the wider community and get their voice heard at national level.

→

The community wanted to go beyond filling gaps in service provision, recognising that a new District Centre had the potential to do more than bring services together in one place. It provided a timely opportunity for the delivery of integrated services through a neighbourhood management approach.

Services in the Centre are entirely community-led and have been developed around the needs of the community rather than organisational boundaries. The services available include a community centre, café, Citizens Advice, youth services, a range of health facilities and a community enterprise centre.

Community asset ownership

One of the important themes of the Local Government White Paper (2006) involves extended opportunities for transferring neighbourhood assets to local communities. The main benefits to communities of taking on asset ownership can be summarised as follows:

- Communities can be given a significant boost and a new pride in where they live – major factors in keeping neighbourhoods successful
- Income and any surpluses generated by the asset are kept within the neighbourhood, with potential 'multiplier effects' for the local economy
- User groups can plan more effectively for the future, with less short-term revenue uncertainty
- Asset ownership is a powerful capacity building tool, helping to broaden and strengthen community skills and experience
- Asset ownership provides both financial and policy leverage for communities interested in greater neighbourhood control. It brings new status and recognition, alongside increased responsibility.

For external agencies, the main benefits of community asset ownership are:

- The potential for giving under-used and/or inadequately resourced facilities a more sustainable future
- The ability to attract additional funds for neighbourhood facilities that are not necessarily available to public sector bodies, potentially turning a financial liability into an asset
- The potential to provide a popular, accessible base for neighbourhood services, particularly in rural areas
- A new incentive for community organisations to work in close partnership with public bodies, helping to make services more responsive to community needs.

Transferring neighbourhood assets to community ownership has not been without its difficulties in recent years. The main issues can be summarised as follows:

- Public bodies have not always been convinced that community organisations have the skills and staying power to manage assets successfully. They can also lack an understanding of the benefits of asset transfer to communities and, as a result, often do not include them in their asset management strategies.

- Until 2003, local authorities lacked the appropriate powers to dispose of their assets at below market value and enter into leases at below market rents. Although that has been largely remedied, the need for most local authorities to realise full market value from any asset disposals, to offset the pressure on council tax, remains a significant constraint.

- Financial clawback rules (now relaxed by the Treasury) have been a further disincentive to transfers, often requiring any profits to be returned to the public body and preventing the asset being used to raise further finance.

- Not all community assets may be appropriate for community ownership – some buildings can be a maintenance liability and costly to run. Larger parks and open spaces may also be problematic, because it is often difficult to generate income to support their running costs. For most local authorities they are a financial liability. Community management may be a better option in some cases.

- The availability of funding for community asset ownership has recently increased, through the Big Lottery's Community Buildings Fund, Adventure Capital Fund and Futurebuilders among others, but community organisations have often lost out to commercial buyers when an asset comes onto the market.

- The support and technical guidance needed for community organisations to take over asset ownership and management has been a major constraint in the past, but is now improving. The Development Trusts Association, for example, now has 350 member organisations and provides advice, support and networking across the country. But there is still a need for more skills, knowledge and support on the ground.

The 2006 Local Government White Paper proposals envisage an expansion of community-owned assets, achieved by a combination of additional funding support, the removal of obstacles to transfer and the use of the community call for action mechanism. There are also plans to make it easier for tenants to set up tenant management organisations to take over the running of the social housing stock in their neighbourhoods. The Quirk Review of Community Asset Management and Ownership was set up following the Local Government White Paper and reported in May 2007. The review called for:

- Authoritative guidance on asset transfers from local authorities to community organisations
- A toolkit on risk assessment and management

- Greater access to expert advice and support
- The involvement of specialist financial intermediaries
- A major campaign to promote good practice.

Communities as housing providers

Housing is the largest asset in neighbourhoods; having control over how it is managed and maintained offers residents the biggest opportunity to have an effective say in what happens in their neighbourhood as a whole. Having a substantial asset and control over the budgets gives residents clout with other service providers. But they need skills and experience, and they need willing partners to help them make it happen and keep it sustainable for the foreseeable future.

The options available to communities interested in having more control over their homes are summarised in the table below. They are covered in much more detail in *Taking Control in Your Community: A Guide for Housing Association Tenants* (Confederation for Co-operative Housing 2003).

	Consultation	Power sharing	Community control	Community ownership
Consultation with your housing provider	✓			
Active community involvement in your housing service	✓	✓		
Estate agreements	✓	✓		
Local management agreement		✓	✓	
Tenant management organisation		✓	✓	
Housing co-operative			✓	✓
Community-based housing association			✓	✓
Community Gateway association			✓	✓
Community Land Trust			✓	✓

Community Gateway is one of the relatively new models and one which is attracting significant interest from policy-makers, tenants and local authorities. On council housing estates, people may feel that they are not consulted or involved in decisions that affect their neighbourhoods, especially the big decisions about the future of the housing service and other services they receive. This can happen even where a council has encouraged involvement – or asked people to vote on the future of their housing.

The starting point for the Community Gateway model is that the future of people's homes must be shaped by the people themselves. Achieving local solutions to local issues requires people to develop the ability and power to identify the concerns they have about their homes and neighbourhoods and act upon them. By the time tenants vote on stock transfer, it often seems like a 'take it or leave it' choice. The Community Gateway model aims to change this by getting people involved at a much earlier stage, so that they can shape the choices, not just vote on them. Tenants can choose how much power they want and when they want it with built-in capacity to increase their level of involvement when they choose. Community self-determination will not happen overnight. It will take time, training, flexibility, balance, motivation and safety nets.

There are now several Community Gateway schemes in progress, all at different stages. The Chartered Institute of Housing has published guidance on setting up a Community Gateway organisation and provided progress bulletins when the scheme was in its early stages (see www.cih.org/gateway).

Community leadership in stock transfers
COMMUNITY GATEWAY, PRESTON

The Preston Community Gateway scheme was the first in the country and followed a successful stock transfer ballot in 2004.

The Community Gateway Association is a not-for-profit community business, meeting the housing needs of people in Preston and the surrounding areas. It is a housing association registered with the Housing Corporation, provides high quality homes and is dedicated to placing tenants and communities at the heart of decision-making. It is also very much about creating friendly communities, where people want to live. Its services include:

- Improving homes and neighbourhoods
- Providing tenancy advice and support
- Helping people to choose a suitable home through choice-based lettings
- A dedicated team tackling anti-social behaviour and its causes
- Collecting rents and other charges and providing debt advice
- Working closely with local communities to build individuals' skills, knowledge and confidence.

→

A network of ten Local Community Areas covering Preston gives tenants and communities the opportunity to make decisions about how local neighbourhoods are run and develop realistic action plans. Seven of the 15 board members are tenants; local people are also represented on the Gateway Tenant Committee, through neighbourhood groups and ongoing, direct contact with staff and other residents. Currently £400,000 each year is available to spend on community empowerment, helping local people get the skills they need to run their services, improving the quality of life for everyone in the community.

Tenants influence the work of the CGA in many ways, including:

- Taking direct responsibility for how some services are delivered to their neighbourhood
- Setting up community organisations, ranging from parent and toddler groups to new businesses
- Developing new links with partners (such as the police) to tackle local issues together.

Resident consultancies

A number of well-established, community-run neighbourhood organisations have now begun to market their skills and experience more widely, through a 'learning through shared experience' process. There is an extensive, unrecognised skills base within most communities. While existing skills and knowledge need bringing out and enhancing, the key attributes may well be there already. The best people to unlock them are often other, more experienced residents rather than professionals.

Government has been encouraging the development of resident consultancies, running a short pilot programme in 2002/3 based around a small number of these organisations, including several good practice case studies featured in this guide. They have now been incorporated into the Guide Neighbourhoods programme.

Turning residents into consultants
HOUSING JUSTICE REGENERATE

A key strategy for creating successful communities involves turning residents into consultants. This has been a challenging, but rewarding aspect of community involvement in service provision, placing communities at the heart of regeneration activities.

→

Housing Justice Regenerate is a community-led regeneration service based on the recognition that residents living and working in their own neighbourhoods 24 hours a day, 7 days a week are essential for the creation of sustainable communities and the delivery of quality public services. Housing Justice Regenerate is grounded in the belief that residents are the best people to lead and sustain the regeneration of their neighbourhoods.

It aims to enable residents who have been through the process of regeneration to share their experiences with others. Expert resident guides are equipped to encourage and inspire other residents to get involved in community regeneration. The programme offers a package of step-by-step, on-the-job learning through regeneration and renewal for existing and future resident leaders.

Turning residents into consultants has been secured by funding from CLG's Community Empowerment division, and is a Guide Neighbourhoods project. www.housingjustice.org.uk

Guide Neighbourhoods are successful community organisations that have tackled issues such as crime, poor housing and unemployment in their community. They are being funded as part of the government's *Together We Can* action plan, to pass on the lessons they have learned to other community groups who want to tackle similar issues in their neighbourhoods. There are 15 Guide Neighbourhoods (listed in appendix C of this guide), all of them strong, successful, resident-led organisations, sharing their knowledge and experience with other neighbourhoods. They are characterised by putting the interests of the community first and never taking 'no' for an answer.

Introducing community wardens across a city
GOODWIN DEVELOPMENT TRUST, HULL

Goodwin Development Trust is a community-led organisation working closely with local residents to develop projects that meet the specific needs of the community. The Trust is part of the Guide Neighbourhood programme. Among its many activities, the Trust has established a highly successful community wardens scheme in Hull. It was the first organisation in the country to set up a community warden project, through a successful bid in 2000 to the Home Office for funding. As a result of the scheme there has been a 50% reduction in crime in the local neighbourhood, a 48% reduction in burglary and 95% of residents now feel safer. The scheme has won several national awards and has now been rolled out to other neighbourhoods across the city.

→

In the pilot neighbourhood, an inner city area to the west of the city centre, residents identified the following issues as priorities: poor environmental conditions, youth disturbances, lack of social inclusion, 'nowhere to meet', high crime figures, widespread fear of crime, anti-social behaviour and racial tensions. To address these issues, highly visible patrols were started to provide reassurance to local residents; equality inclusion wardens were appointed to liaise between asylum seekers, local help groups and counselling services; work with young people was prioritised, with wardens helping to establish youth forums and diversion activities. A Junior Warden Scheme has been particularly successful.

Residents in other neighbourhoods can:

- Visit a Guide Neighbourhood to find out what they have done and how they did it
- Develop a long-term relationship with the Guide Neighbourhood which can offer ongoing advice to help improve the quality of life in their community
- Apply for a small grant to kick start or accelerate the work in their neighbourhood.

Community leadership

Community leaders or activists are a vital resource for delivering the neighbourhood agenda. Their role is usually to:

- Speak up for their community
- Champion the diversity of community views
- Work closely with professionals in their neighbourhood
- Raise difficult issues.

They sit on neighbourhood partnership boards, run tenants' and residents' associations, chair the local community centre management committee and find themselves co-opted onto all sorts of more strategic bodies. They are much in demand. The spotlight is on them and they are under intense pressure to deliver real change in their neighbourhoods. But it was not always so. Over the last 30 years or so community leaders have gone from being demonised, to being patronised and now to being almost eulogised by many professionals and politicians.

Most of these people are grossly over-worked, constantly under stress and desperately under-resourced. Few people would choose to spend 40 or even 50 hours a week running a community centre in a deprived neighbourhood, chairing a community partnership board, coping with constant aggravation and even intimidation, unable to leave it all behind when they go home – and do it all on an entirely voluntary basis.

Such people are true community champions. They often get a real boost from doing something positive for their community and learning new skills. They are well used to consultation fatigue, but many of them are in danger of burn-out. They certainly need more resources, not only to keep them going, but also to spread the load and broaden the base in their neighbourhoods. They are crucial to the success of the neighbourhood agenda.

CHAPTER 7

PUTTING IT INTO PRACTICE – WHAT SHOULD HOUSING PROVIDERS DO?

This chapter of the guide focuses on how housing providers can put into practice the themes of the earlier chapters. It makes the business case for much greater involvement in neighbourhoods and their sustainability, encouraging housing associations and ALMOs to broaden their role to become neighbourhood champions and enablers.

It includes good practice advice on resourcing neighbourhoods, stock rationalisation, managing mixed-tenure neighbourhoods and encouraging community cohesion. Finally, it looks at how housing providers should gear themselves up for change and evaluate the outcomes, to ensure they have a major role in delivering the neighbourhood agenda.

The business case for the neighbourhood agenda

The new agenda for neighbourhoods is ambitious. Its success, and the success of many deprived neighbourhoods themselves depends, in no small measure, on housing providers taking the lead. Some already are, but there is more to be done. Housing associations, in particular, have a key role to play.

The National Housing Federation's iN business for neighbourhoods initiative makes the case for a much more robust involvement by housing providers in the neighbourhood agenda. Its goal is to unify the sector, enabling it to create successful neighbourhoods where people want to live and challenge negative perceptions of housing associations and their customers. It urges participating housing associations to:

- Exercise a wider neighbourhood regeneration role and play a part in tackling residents' liveability issues, irrespective of their tenure
- Work more closely in partnership with other housing associations, local authorities and other key service providers

- Disseminate models of good practice to counter negative perceptions and misconceptions
- Actively decide whether they are best suited to providing a lead or supporting role
- Consider relinquishing stock in areas where they have no real role to play
- Ensure that they are getting right the basics of delivering high quality housing and management
- Be open, accountable and transparent organisations and work well with others, especially residents and local authorities.

Since its launch in 2003, around 600 housing associations with 1.75 million homes have signed up to iN business. There has been a lot invested in the initiative. But it does not yet go far enough and there are doubts about whether many housing providers currently have the capacity, as well as the appetite, to deal with the neighbourhood agenda in all its aspects.

Involvement in non-housing issues in neighbourhoods is increasing steadily, but is still largely confined to bigger housing associations and those that are community based or controlled. Only 3% of them are officially classified by the Housing Corporation as 'diverse' organisations and less than one in five undertake any non-housing activities at all. For many, involvement in non-housing activities is primarily about strengthening their core business, by reducing voids and rent arrears or strengthening demand for their stock. These are important drivers, but they are not, in themselves, likely to place these housing providers at the forefront of the neighbourhood agenda. There is much to learn from those housing providers that have gone much further.

In comparison with activities that show immediate results, it can be difficult for housing organisations to rely on the longer-term benefits offered by focusing on neighbourhoods. The section at the end of this chapter gives details on demonstrating progress in this area, but meanwhile it is worth examining 'the business case' more closely. For social housing providers, it is possible to identify six aspects which comprise the business case:

- Organisational
- Financial
- Social
- Community
- Ethical / moral
- Political – ability to influence locally, regionally and nationally.

These points together, and the relative priority given to each of them by the organisation for its areas of operation, will help to focus on adopting genuinely neighbourhood objectives, and give part of the framework for assessing progress against each of these headings. For example, on page 119 the box on the rewards of neighbourhood management lists many areas which would support the viability of a housing provider's business. Part of the consideration of the business case, is to consider the significant risks associated with giving insufficient priority to supporting neighbourhoods. It is important to protect previous investment and asset values, particularly by contributing to the prevention of neighbourhood decline and keeping management costs down.

The Housing Corporation's Neighbourhoods and Communities Strategy, launched in October 2006, also encourages registered housing associations – and by extension ALMOs – to put neighbourhoods at the heart of their thinking and future activities, lifting some of the previous restrictions on how much of their business can be focused on non-housing activities. The strategy covers five key areas:

1. **Working together** – outlining how the Housing Corporation sees housing associations, local authorities and others working together in partnership to deliver for local communities.
2. **Sustaining mixed communities** – setting out how the Corporation and housing associations can contribute to delivering and sustaining successful, mixed communities.
3. **Adding community value** – highlighting the growing role of housing associations as social entrepreneurs and neighbourhood-level delivery agents, in addition to their core housing role.
4. **Building Respect** – detailing the critical role of housing associations in tackling anti-social behaviour and delivering the Respect agenda.
5. **Empowering communities** – highlighting the critical importance of residents and communities informing the work of housing associations and holding them to account.

Housing Corporation endorsement of the neighbourhood agenda is important; it sets a clear strategic direction, based on acceptance of the business case for a wider role for housing providers in neighbourhoods. The test will be how it is implemented and the level of encouragement and incentives that are provided to further extend the good work that is already happening on the ground.

So how ready are housing providers for their new or extended role? Despite major reorganisations and mergers in recent years, housing associations still come in many different shapes and sizes. Collectively, they have many strengths and weaknesses.

THE NEIGHBOURHOOD AGENDA
HOUSING ASSOCIATION STRENGTHS

Housing associations have many strengths to bring to delivering the neighbourhood agenda, including their:

- **Diversity:** there are many types and sizes, including some large group structures
- **Creativity:** the best associations are innovative and flexible
- **Financial strength:** larger associations have the ability to re-invest surpluses in neighbourhood services
- **Risk assessment skills**
- **Project management skills**
- **Experience In meeting specialist needs**
- **High rates of tenant satisfaction** with the services they provide
- **Long-term stakeholding in neighbourhoods,** giving them an ability to plan ahead
- **Links between housing management and street services,** providing scope to support or even lead on neighbourhood management
- **Regular contact with residents,** their local knowledge and frequently trust
- **Track record in regeneration and renewal**
- **Independence,** non-political nature, and their freedom to act speedily compared with local authorities and other statutory service providers
- **Advocacy role** in pressing the case of neglected areas
- **Regulated status** so communities know standards will be met.

THE NEIGHBOURHOOD AGENDA
HOUSING ASSOCIATION WEAKNESSES

Alongside its strengths, the housing association sector also has a number of weaknesses affecting its ability to deliver the neighbourhood agenda, including the following:

- Associations remain **heavily regulated** by the Housing Corporation
- Although many are keen to operate on a broader basis in neighbourhoods, they also need **to get the basics right and deliver their core business** – increased efficiency in delivering additional homes and decent homes targets
- **Rent restructuring** limits their scope to finance wider action from rental income
- **Local authority nomination agreements** can sometimes frustrate efforts to create mixed, sustainable, communities

→

- Housing associations often have **properties spread over many different neighbourhoods,** and therefore their management lacks a neighbourhood focus
- Some are **reluctant to concede a lead management role,** even to another housing association
- There is still a **development bias** in some associations; management performance and a wider role in neighbourhoods is often seen as of secondary importance
- Social housing has an **image problem** with some policy-makers, politicians and communities
- Housing associations are often not closely involved in **Local Strategic Partnerships**
- There has been **under-exploitation of neighbourhood funding opportunities,** including the Neighbourhood Renewal Fund and the Safer and Stronger Communities Fund
- **Competition** between associations gives a fragmented rather than united feel to the sector
- **Tenant consultation is still tokenistic** in some associations
- The **iN business for neighbourhoods challenge** has not been implemented by some housing associations
- There are **capacity issues for very small housing associations** with a limited housing stock.

Housing providers that have genuinely embraced the neighbourhood agenda tend to share a core philosophy which goes a little beyond the approach of many of their peers:

- A willingness to provide more than just housing services if necessary
- A commitment to extend tenant engagement and also community capacity building
- A concern for tenants' wider welfare
- A focus on consumer needs and outcomes rather than service providers' interests
- A sense of social responsibility to the wider community
- A desire to work in genuine partnership with other associations, housing organisations and key local service providers.

But, as already set out at the end of chapter 3, there is much more that can and should be done if housing providers are to maximise their strengths, tackle their weaknesses and really focus on their neighbourhoods.

Many housing associations began life as small voluntary organisations, but time has changed them so much that they are now largely unrecognisable as such. They have become complex, highly professional businesses with significant assets and turnovers. England's largest association now has an annual turnover of £255 million and assets of £2.3 billion. The challenge for these associations is to use their long experience and financial muscle to deliver the neighbourhood agenda. One way of doing so is to reconnect with their roots.

G15 HOUSING ASSOCIATIONS, LONDON

G15 is a group of leading housing associations in London managing over 60% of the capital's half a million housing association homes. In 2004, the group commissioned an independent report *Social Capital* which examined its members' contribution to meeting government targets for improving Londoners' quality of life. It showed that housing associations do not simply deliver low-cost housing and physical regeneration, but a wide range of employment, health, education and community safety initiatives. At that stage, G15 associations had:

- Initiated or supported 534 people-based projects since 1997, investing nearly £100 million
- Spent £18 million on 51 neighbourhood planning and renewal projects
- Accessed 15 different non-housing funding sources to support its community investment work
- Spent £26 million on community capacity building and social exclusion.

The G15 has supported the development of new networks and promoted skills bases on estates and in the areas in which they operate. They are enabling diverse communities to engage in decision-making and to help themselves. The G15 is responding across the board to the neighbourhood agenda.

Developing neighbourhood hubs

There is potential for some housing providers to become 'community anchors' in neighbourhoods. Recent research for Hact and the National Housing Federation has demonstrated that the best of them have already:

- Invested heavily in the poorest neighbourhoods
- Committed themselves to remaining in these neighbourhoods
- Adapted their tenant consultation processes to encompass the wider community
- Developed expertise in linking housing investment with support for local economies
- Helped establish sustainable community and social enterprises
- Shared staff and facilities to provide a comprehensive neighbourhood service.

Housing providers have much to learn from the locally-based community and voluntary sector organisations which have everyday experience of how their neighbourhoods work. Some housing associations – large and relatively small – are now involved in developing neighbourhood hubs, working closely with the voluntary and community sectors to build relationships and develop new, powerful ways of working.

But contributing to successful neighbourhoods is about more than working in new and imaginative ways with voluntary and community groups. It is also about new forms of delivery – housing providers using their skills and knowledge to facilitate community ownership and management of neighbourhood assets, helping establish community-based housing organisations through stock rationalisation and signing up to neighbourhood charters. There is much to do.

WHAT CAN HOUSING PROVIDERS DO TO SUPPORT THE NEIGHBOURHOOD AGENDA?

- Get directly involved in the neighbourhood agenda at strategic level, not just in neighbourhoods themselves; become active partners in Local Area Agreements and Local Strategic Partnerships
- Take the lead, with others, on developing special purpose vehicles (SPVs) to deliver neighbourhood change
- Keep staff and offices as local as possible, based in neighbourhoods with significant stock holdings and/or regeneration activity
- Rationalise housing management, or even stock ownership, focusing on specific neighbourhoods, and transferring management or stock to other providers where appropriate
- Establish neighbourhood budgets for housing management services and devolve specific responsibilities to neighbourhood staff
- Play a prominent role in setting up and supporting neighbourhood governance arrangements
- Build the strength of tenants, to ensure they play a full role in neighbourhood arrangements and encourage them to work closely with owner occupiers, leaseholders and others in the community
- Encourage tenants to explore options for taking on the management of their homes and help with setting up a tenant management organisation
- Facilitate the transfer of the management and, where possible, the ownership of local assets (including housing) to neighbourhood bodies, where appropriate
- Sign up to neighbourhood charters

→

- Play a lead role in delivering the Respect agenda in neighbourhoods, by taking positive action against anti-social tenants in their stock and providing financial or other support to neighbourhood wardens
- Invest in community priorities for neighbourhood facilities and activities
- Introduce local letting schemes and tenure change initiatives, to encourage more mixed communities on mono-tenure estates.

Resourcing the neighbourhood

Widening the housing provider role in neighbourhoods is not a cost-free activity; it needs to be properly resourced. Because the costs often arise in the short-term and the benefits usually take longer to come through, making a strong case is not always straightforward.

Some housing providers have expressed concerns that, as custodians of their tenants' money, paid through rents, they have an obligation to ensure that spending is focused on meeting their needs and not necessarily those of the wider community. While this is a valid concern, it misunderstands the real needs and aspirations of tenants and the importance of an holistic approach to neighbourhoods. It may even be used by some organisations as a smokescreen for keeping activities within the 'comfort zone' of traditional housing management. It is no coincidence that many of the country's tenant-controlled housing associations have been among the leaders in broadening their neighbourhood and community role.

Although neighbourhood activity can take many forms, resourcing neighbourhood management is likely to represent the biggest challenge for many housing providers. While they are unlikely to be the only service provider facing a resource requirement, their lead role in regeneration activities and their often extensive stock holding in neighbourhoods means they may be expected to make a significant contribution, at least initially.

Achieving value for money through neighbourhood management

Those housing providers with experience of resourcing neighbourhood management have generally found that the following activities represent good value for money, delivering added value from their investment of staff time and funding:

- Initial small scale, short term **'quick wins'** projects which raise the profile and credibility of programmes, counter disenchantment with existing services and previous initiatives, inspire residents and boost community confidence (eg neighbourhood wardens, clean-up programmes, CCTV).

- **Multi-purpose buildings** featuring service co-location and space for community organisations which can generate a great deal of energy, self-help and commitment from the local community, especially if they can be locally run.

- **Financial support for small-scale community projects**, involving comparatively modest sums of money, which boost local confidence (eg community grants schemes) and joint initiatives with the private sector (eg new local cash points and retail facilities).

THE COSTS AND BENEFITS OF NEIGHBOURHOOD MANAGEMENT FOR HOUSING PROVIDERS

The costs

- Employing or funding a neighbourhood manager and team
- Upfront investment in a local office, equipment etc
- Additional maintenance, cleaning and security services
- Building and maintaining links with residents and community groups
- Establishing and servicing a neighbourhood management steering group or Board
- Securing local authority political backing and central support/re-orientation
- Dialogue/co-ordination work with other key service providers (eg the police)
- Additional revenue costs for deployment of additional frontline staff
- Collection of additional neighbourhood intelligence on needs and services.

Anticipated benefits and rewards

- Greater sense of pride and commitment to an area, better environmental conditions and potentially lower maintenance and repair costs
- More patrolling, supervision and control over neighbourhood conditions
- More resident input and liaison
- More reporting, more local information, better informed action
- Better co-ordination and understanding between local stakeholders
- Innovative projects and initiatives
- More investment in neighbourhood businesses and households, leading to greater asset appreciation
- Reduced tenancy turnover and fewer voids, providing a stronger income base
- More positive interest in the neighbourhood from senior local authority politicians and officers, creating a virtuous circle
- Skill development for residents, with greater access to training and local job creation, therefore boosting the local economy.

Sharing the resourcing role

Housing providers will normally expect to share the resourcing role in neighbourhoods with other service providers – particularly local authorities and perhaps the police – but individual providers rarely have a monopoly of the social housing stock in any large neighbourhood. In many cases, a co-ordinated, cohesive approach to neighbourhoods, through joint working between different housing providers, can help spread the load, enabling them to pool resources and ideas, improve the value-for-money calculations and deliver more than the sum of their joint parts. Ways in which this can be achieved include the following:

- Joint marketing
- Joint asset management planning
- Joint procurement and management policies
- Stock rationalisation.

There is growing experience of joint working in neighbourhoods between different housing providers, nowhere more so than on Merseyside, where some important pioneering work is under way. Here, it is not uncommon for up to ten housing associations to own and manage stock in a single neighbourhood. Now, these associations are looking at more rational ways of owning and managing the social housing stock in these neighbourhoods, and contributing to the neighbourhood agenda – both to strengthen their businesses and better meet the needs and aspirations of local communities. The LIFE model has been further developed through the local strategic partnership.

The housing association experience in Liverpool and elsewhere can be widely adopted to improve coordination and joint approaches in neighbourhoods. ALMOs, local authority housing departments and stock transfer associations can all rationalise the way they work together in neighbourhoods, alongside other housing providers.

LIVERPOOL'S LIFE MODEL

Housing associations are playing a leading role in housing market renewal in Liverpool, where they own or manage 15% of the housing stock, rising to 26% in the inner core of the city. Their participation in housing market renewal and neighbourhood management is crucial.

The LIFE model is a blueprint for partnership working developed by Liverpool City Council and its Strategic Housing Partnership. The model enables collaboration and cooperation between the city, housing associations and key stakeholders by providing a structured approach to the management of areas of opportunity.

→

The core principle is that the combined contribution of stakeholders creates the conditions for vibrant and stable communities. In this way LIFE differs from other approaches to rationalisation that have focused on the ownership of stock rather than the management of an area.

The housing market renewal area includes four Zones of Opportunity or ZOOs, with associations taking one of the following roles in each of them:

- **Lead** – where the agreed association working with the city council and main private developer take the lead in delivering housing market renewal

- **Influence** – where associations with commitment and interest in a zone or with specialist skills, work with others to influence what happens

- **Follow** – where associations collaborate to deliver the strategic direction set by the lead organisation

- **Exit** – where associations who see no longer-term management or development opportunities make a strategic decision to withdraw from a zone.

Each zone has a LIFE forum that brings together the partner associations and other stakeholders to produce and implement neighbourhood management and redevelopment schemes. The City organises a city-wide LIFE Forum at which the four lead associations meet on a quarterly basis to discuss the operation of the model across the four zones.

The model offers a number of benefits:
- Clarity of planning and communications
- Coordinated delivery and efficiencies through joint working
- Increased and more effective community involvement.

The LIFE model's achievements include:
- Better housing options for households affected by renewal
- Joint action on anti-social behaviour
- Action to support diversity including bilingual staff in accessible offices
- New affordable housing giving increased tenure choice
- Handypersons scheme
- Stock rationalisation
- Improved neighbourhood management and better, more inclusive services.

Rationalising the neighbourhood housing stock

All housing associations have been urged to examine their patterns of property ownership and management to ensure they meet key policy objectives. CIH's 2007 report *The Rationalisation of Housing Association Stock* shows that widely dispersed housing stock, remoteness of housing managers from tenants, and multi-landlord estates can all lead to poor service to residents, lack of involvement in neighbourhoods and higher costs to housing providers. It also highlights the critical strategic role of local authorities in developing rationalisation strategies where this is appropriate. The Housing Corporation's *Rationalisation Guide and Toolkit* supports housing associations in putting theory into practice.

The neighbourhood agenda, as expressed in the Local Government White Paper 2006, encourages an expansion of community asset ownership. Although the precise mechanisms are still being developed, this important emphasis means that stock rationalisation might usefully go further than neighbourhood stock swaps between existing housing associations. Helping to create new community-led organisations to take on stock should now be firmly on the agenda as an option.

Stock rationalisation is not all plain sailing, however. There are a number of potential barriers, including the following:

- Rationalisation is time consuming and complex to achieve, needing significant resources, particularly staff time, to make it happen. Inertia may mean that there is no significant activity.
- There are important, unresolved cultural issues to overcome. Many housing associations are geared to growth and most do not want to reduce their stock (and for smaller associations losing properties can undermine their financial health).
- Working in a particular local authority area, no matter how small the stock holding, makes it easier to gain approval for new development there.
- Management agreements have VAT implications for housing associations.
- Breaking up the ownership and management of large housing stocks into many smaller community-based organisations may impact on value for money and economies of scale unless joint procurement and maintenance arrangements are put in place.

A key question is whether stock rationalisation, in whatever form, helps to create and sustain successful neighbourhoods, or is simply a new mechanism for strengthening housing association business plans and enabling them to manage their assets more efficiently. Both are clearly important and need to be factored into decision-making processes.

Changing mono-tenure areas

There has been a widespread assumption in recent years that changing the pattern of tenure – and by extension, incomes – on many social housing estates is one of the keys to delivering successful neighbourhoods. It can help provide a boost to the local economy, tackle entrenched deprivation and improve social and community facilities.

Breaking up estates, by demolishing unpopular types of housing and building new homes for sale and shared ownership has undoubtedly contributed to the successful regeneration of many places, but it is only one factor. How a neighbourhood looks and feels, its location and the type and quality of local services (particularly the quality of local schools) are all equally important.

FROM MONO-TENURE TO MIXED TENURE NEIGHBOURHOODS

MAKING THE CHANGE

- Tenure change existing and future empty homes (including 'trickle transfers' for shared ownership)
- Remodel existing small homes to create larger ones for sale
- Carry out selective demolition and change layouts to meet buyers' modern needs and aspirations
- Provide a range of tenures in new replacement homes
- Develop and monitor sales and lettings plans to reflect demographic and income changes over time
- Establish new partnerships to generate local job opportunities, to retain a buoyant local economy and keep wage-earners in the neighbourhood
- Support and facilitate a range of neighbourhood interventions, including neighbourhood management, to improve and sustain the social and community infrastructure.

JRF-sponsored research, published by CIH, into the role mixed tenure can play in creating and sustaining successful neighbourhoods showed that outcomes are generally positive, although there are inevitably downsides:

- Mixed income communities are generally successful; they are not characterised by the problems often linked with exclusively low-income areas. They seem to meet the expectations of developers, residents and housing managers and have generally become more pleasant places to live, learn and work.

- Mixed tenure and mixed income are not an issue to most residents – they see their neighbours as 'ordinary people'. While residents may not develop personal friendships across tenures, they describe their relationships as 'civil' and 'polite'.

- Mixed income communities can help attract young families back to inner urban areas by providing more appropriate housing, especially if there is also an improvement in the quality of local schools.

- Developers involved in mixed tenure developments appear to have few major problems. There is no evidence that mixed communities lower the price of houses for sale or put off potential purchasers. Design, location and quality – not tenure – are seen as the key factors affecting sales and price levels.

- Planning tenure mix is only one part of the picture. Tenure is not fixed and, as it alters in a community, so can the population of residents. On one large estate monitored by an LSE long-term study, half the homes converted from social renting to home ownership had subsequently switched to private renting – prices fell as owners moved out, forcing some to rent their homes out to repay the mortgage.

- There is little evidence so far that mixed tenure breaks down barriers between different income groups, delivers more social cohesion or improves the image of neighbourhoods; people do not change their lifestyle to reflect that of their neighbours.

- There are also tensions between tenure change and the ability of housing providers to continue meeting an increasingly diverse range of housing needs.

Changing any estate from mono to mixed tenure is certainly not a panacea, but it does have an important role to play in making deprived urban neighbourhoods more successful.

CHANGING THE FACE OF EAST LEEDS

Leeds City Council's East and South East Leeds (EASEL) initiative is a joint venture with Bellway plc to regenerate some of the most deprived neighbourhoods in the city. At least 120 hectares of council-owned land will be developed for new housing and other complementary uses, including local services and amenities to improve life for residents. The whole programme could take up to 15 years, bringing in substantial private sector investment and changing the face of inner east Leeds.

79,000 people live in the EASEL area; 19 neighbourhoods here are within the 3% most deprived Super Output Areas in the country.

→

The EASEL objectives include:

- Improving local skill levels and employment opportunities
- Raising incomes for households
- Providing new, higher quality homes for people wishing to live in the area
- Providing choice in housing tenure
- Improving the quality of the environment
- Improving the attractiveness of the area for new homebuyers and increasing land values
- Attracting new investment into the area to improve the economy of this part of inner East Leeds and its relationship to the city as a whole.

EASEL is not a stand-alone initiative. It will be linked to other important development opportunities and regeneration programmes in east and south east Leeds.

The first phase of EASEL is focused on the Gipton and Seacroft neighbourhoods. Work on the development of 750 new homes here is expected to take five years. Gipton has been designated a 'Mixed Community' pilot area by the government; it is mainly an area of council housing with high crime levels, low skills and low educational attainment. In addition to the mixed tenure housing schemes, the first steps towards developing a mixed community here will include measures to improve skills and pre-work training and are being delivered through:

- A newly-established local base
- A project to improve family income (which includes outreach workers who are working with families to address debt, benefit take-up and employment support)
- The recent introduction of an intensive neighbourhood management programme.

Choice-based lettings

Choice-based lettings (CBL) schemes are a way of giving tenants a greater say over where they live when social tenancies are allocated. The aim of CBL is to have more satisfied tenants, who stay longer, pay the rent and look after their homes, delivering in turn more stable, viable and inclusive communities and more successful neighbourhoods. Initial research indicates that CBL is successful, including improving BME applicants' access to more areas.

Around one-quarter of local authorities have set up choice-based lettings schemes so far – many in partnership with housing associations – and their spread is a key part of the drive to create and sustain successful neighbourhoods.

Supporting stronger, more cohesive communities

Unless a package of neighbourhood initiatives also succeeds in building more cohesive communities, where people interact with each other in positive ways, respect their differences and expand their informal networks, many neighbourhoods will still struggle to be successful.

Chapter 4 provided an overview of community cohesion and the overriding importance of bringing diverse communities together if many of our inner city neighbourhoods are to become successful for the long term. Research by CIH concluded that housing providers should be playing a key role in helping to deliver this part of the neighbourhood agenda, by:

- Creating more mixed neighbourhoods and diversifying existing ones
- Creating new opportunities for black and minority ethnic communities to live in neighbourhoods outside their existing settlement areas
- Recognising that 'engineering' neighbourhoods where people from different backgrounds live side-by-side is not enough to deliver community cohesion
- Confronting racist harassment wherever and however it occurs in any neighbourhood
- Acting as role models by diversifying their own practices, their governance arrangements and the involvement of people from different backgrounds in their activities
- Promoting and supporting a range of inter-community activities and networking
- Building bridges with new black and minority ethnic communities, including refugees and asylum seekers, and migrants from EU accession states
- Focusing involvement on young people
- Encouraging segregated communities to work together on projects of mutual benefit.

In practical terms, housing providers also need to ask themselves the following questions in relation to community cohesion:

- Are you aware of issues and/or community concerns that could ignite tensions in the neighbourhoods where you have stock?
- Who in the neighbourhood is not engaging?
- Are you in regular contact with community and faith leaders?

- Are there problems with disaffected young people?
- Are there issues with extreme political or religious activity operating locally?
- Are neighbourhoods in which you operate experiencing 'white flight' and 'wealth flight'?
- Do you have contingency plans to manage inflammatory press coverage about community tensions effectively?
- Is planning for community cohesion part of your business plan?

The honest answers to these and other questions should form the basis for a housing provider's community cohesion strategy, a key part of its neighbourhood agenda.

Delivering the Respect agenda

The government's Respect programme is a broad and cross-cutting response to anti-social behaviour and its causes, and as such it sits well with the wider neighbourhood agenda. It recognises that community engagement is central and that making services better at managing behaviour – tackling bad and promoting good – is crucially linked to delivering on issues such as social justice and child poverty. The Respect agenda aims to:

- Provide more and better support for families
- Take a new, interventionist approach with the most challenging families
- Improve behaviour and attendance in schools
- Provide more activities for children and young people in their neighbourhoods
- Invest in strengthening communities so they are better able to tackle some of the problems themselves
- Provide effective enforcement and community justice.

Housing providers play a key part in delivering the Respect agenda. They need to develop a balanced and proportionate approach to tackling anti-social behaviour and crime – one that offers strategies for prevention, intervention, support and enforcement. They can:

- Sign up to the government's Respect Standard for Housing Management
- Develop and implement an anti-social behaviour strategy, supported by practical, outcome-focused policies and procedures
- Widely publicise their approach to tackling anti-social behaviour to all local residents (not just tenants)
- Involve local communities directly in delivering the strategy on a neighbourhood basis

- Support community calls for action where these involve anti-social behaviour issues

- Respond quickly to anti-social behaviour events over which they have control as a landlord, with robust enforcement and appropriate publicity

- Employ or contribute to the costs of neighbourhood and community wardens, CCTV coverage and other anti-social behaviour measures, once agreed with the local community

- Play an active role in Crime and Disorder Reduction Partnerships and develop and maintain other operational partnerships with key agencies

- Make use of acceptable behaviour contracts and parenting contracts to tackle anti-social behaviour at source

- Help establish diversionary activities and facilities for young people

- Work closely with the community and voluntary sector to strengthen their engagement with young people

- Celebrate and share success.

40 Respect Areas were chosen by the government in early 2007, where communities had already shown a determination to tackle anti-social behaviour. At the same time, local authorities were given the ability to devolve powers to apply for Anti-Social Behaviour Orders (ASBOs) to ALMOs and tenant management organisations.

Gearing up for change

So far, this chapter has focused on activities that housing providers can undertake to help deliver successful neighbourhoods. But delivery is not just dependent on a range of external activities; it also requires change in the way things are done internally.

Over the past few years many housing providers have put a lot of effort into reorganising the way they do things, changing their board and staffing structures, setting up new teams and retraining old ones and generally equipping themselves to tackle a raft of new agendas, not just the neighbourhood one. Most would agree, however, that there is more to be done to ensure they are fully geared up for putting the neighbourhood agenda into practice.

CIH and the Academy for Sustainable Communities (ASC) have established a partnership to ensure that housing professionals working in neighbourhoods develop the necessary generic skills such as community engagement, leadership, project management and partnership working.

Cultural change

If there is a 'missing link' in the way housing providers have been gearing up for the neighbourhood agenda, it has to do with empowering communities. Recent research suggests that communities only have a real say in the services and decisions that affect their daily lives in neighbourhoods if local authorities, housing providers and other public bodies have changed their internal systems and working culture, to make sure it happens.

Some organisations have made significant progress in this respect, but overall not enough has yet changed. In many neighbourhoods, residents remain at a disadvantage in their relationships with housing providers, even where there is a corporate will to engage. Interest in community empowerment is often confined, in practical terms, to relatively junior staff employed by housing providers; senior staff have traditionally been required to have different attributes and priorities. There is often a reluctance to 'let go' at local level. Community empowerment requires a lot of 'letting go', with all the risks and potential benenfits that accompanies it.

A submission from the Confederation for Co-operative Housing to the National Housing Federation's Tenant Involvement Commission suggested that housing providers need to make a number of important changes to their structures and practices if community empowerment is to become a reality:

- Chief executives should be responsible for their association's community empowerment strategies (with dedicated staff responsible for delivery)

- The most senior member of staff responsible for delivery of community empowerment functions should be recruited by and accountable to tenants (in partnership with the chief executive) and should be seen as an integral part of senior management teams

- All members of staff, including senior management team members, should have community empowerment specified in their job descriptions and receive training about what this means

- Tenants' views should be included in all board papers as a matter of course, in the same way that housing providers list equal opportunities and financial considerations

- Tenants should be involved in some way (as tenants, not as board members) with the recruitment of the chief executive and senior management teams, and boards need to consider tenants' views when making decisions about who to employ.

These are radical proposals and would be seen as such by most housing providers, but they offer a useful pointer to what needs to change if the neighbourhood agenda is going to be delivered successfully and not merely paid lip service by housing providers.

Capacity building

Changing the culture in organisations, to bring the neighbourhood agenda to the forefront of organisational thinking and action is not just about how things are done, but also about who is doing them, their skills, experience and attitudes. Internal capacity building is a critical component of cultural change – and not just for frontline staff and board members; chief executives and senior management need it too.

Every housing provider should develop an internal capacity building plan, which should include the following components:

- A vision and commitment to change, agreed at board and executive level
- Interpretation and implementation on a day-to-day basis by senior staff
- Organisational restructuring to change from departmental issue-based working, to multi-disciplinary neighbourhood-based working
- An organisational capacity building plan, defining what gaps/weaknesses need addressing and what strengths need building on
- An organisational development plan detailing the learning, training and skills needs of all staff and board/executive members, including a requirement for key staff to experience working on the front line
- Development of an open access plan, to encourage residents into the organisation, build confidence and understanding
- Development of a diversity action plan, covering service delivery and employment practices
- Individual professional development plans, to ensure career progression for neighbourhood-based staff
- A review of staff composition and levels to ensure that frontline staff have the necessary status and remuneration
- A menu of incentives to encourage all staff to tailor their approach to the neighbourhood agenda
- A review of committee/board structures, to ensure strong representation by neighbourhood representatives.

Evaluating impacts and outcomes

Evaluating impacts and outcomes is important. Not enough of it is done and even when it is, it is not always done in the right way. Changing the way things are done and focusing on something new are usually challenging and sometimes unpredictable; they carry an element of risk. For any organisation, it is always important to take a step back and look closely at the impacts and outcomes; knowing what works, for whom, in what circumstances and why provides valuable evidence for continuing as planned or making changes. It informs decision-making.

The basics of how most organisations do this are well known:

- Defining the aims and objectives of the evaluation
- Establishing a baseline
- Agreeing indicators and targets
- Collecting and analysing the information
- Disseminating the outcomes.

What is harder for housing providers is identifying a process which reflects the key principles of neighbourhood working (community involvement, reconfigured services, etc) and effectively measures the various elements, many of which are intangible.

Trying to identify good models for evaluating neighbourhood working is difficult; successful evaluations at local level are rare. National evaluations of the neighbourhood management pathfinders have, however, produced a wealth of information, both quantitative and qualitative, providing plenty of evidence about the conditions and circumstances necessary for its success.

Doing it better – principles and approaches

Evaluation is most effective when it:

- Is a continuous (not just one-off) process, informing planning and delivery over the life of an initiative
- Involves all those with an interest in the project in deciding the questions they want answered
- Uses imaginative and creative approaches, which engage those involved
- Helps organisations to be accountable to the wider community
- Is used to challenge discriminatory and oppressive policies and practice, and to overcome inequality and disadvantage
- Highlights and celebrates successes and achievements
- Encourages an honest appraisal of progress, in order to learn from what hasn't worked as well as what has.

Successful evaluation along these lines needs an overall approach and specific methods which focus on the activities and impacts resulting from the co-ordination of a range of agencies and service providers, not just looking at one provider or set of actions. Essentially, it's about finding ways of assessing how change and improvement actually happens in the round. This needs approaches and methods which:

- Are comprehensive and qualitative as well as quantitative
- Are varied and accessible

- Focus on communities as key beneficiaries – followed by local service providers and then strategic agencies and funders
- Measure perceptual impacts – feelings and opinions
- Assess processes – ways of working – as well as outcomes
- Set indicators (measures) which link to relevant local strategies and national targets.

Doing it with feeling – involving local people

The new emphasis on measuring feeling and perception is an important part of evaluation, requiring the direct involvement of local people in all aspects of the process. Some organisations, particularly those in the community and voluntary sector, have been doing this for years. It has not, however, been part of the evaluation mainstream; it should be. Ways in which it might be achieved include:

- Involvement in defining the approach and methods to be used
- Carrying out part of the evaluation, such as assembling baseline information, by undertaking surveys and facilitating discussions
- Shadowing of professional evaluation staff by local residents.

Specific methods which could be used include:

- **Case studies**, stories about particular issues from real life experience
- **Attitude and behaviour statements**, completed at regular intervals (say, every year) and based on questions focused on people's day-to-day experience, with the aim of measuring change in their attitudes and behaviours
- **Video portraits**, short films presenting views and stories
- **Life stories**, expressing feelings and experiences
- **Time lines**, reflecting personal experience over time
- **Photo shoots**, recording views of the neighbourhood
- **Picture galleries**, reflecting images of the neighbourhood.

Many of these methods are particularly useful for drawing out the experiences and views of rarely-heard groups. They can also have the added value effect of generating discussions and events outside the evaluative process, which can have a beneficial impact on community capacity and cohesion.

Things can only get worse – the progress paradox

Happiness, both individual and collective, is now widely recognised as a key determinant of social stability and satisfaction. It is a vital factor in the success of any neighbourhood and should be a key indicator in any evaluation.

However, a change in the way things are done will not always lead to short or even medium term increases in satisfaction, even though it may well deliver the very things that communities say they want. Improved physical and material circumstances do not necessarily make people feel happier. This is often called 'the progress paradox', where even though the quality of life is getting better when measured on the usual indicators, people can feel worse – at least in the short term.

There are often clear reasons for this:

- As conditions in the neighbourhood improve, people's expectations rise (they expect more) and change (they expect to feel better, not just see things getting better around them)
- Residents are not convinced that the improvements will last, perhaps based on neighbourhood history which has led to scepticism
- Change, even if positive, can result in anxiety and insecurity
- Individual benefit from the improvements in the neighbourhood is less clear or widely felt than community benefit.

More specifically:

- A changing population will almost inevitably increase uncertainty and fear
- If community cohesion is already fragile it can be further destabilised by change
- Crime figures may fall but residents are likely to be increasingly concerned about anti-social behaviour
- Due to limited resources, work may be focused on certain key areas (for example crime and safety, the environment and housing) and other areas (say, young people and health) might get worse.

Fundamentally, new approaches, and none more so than neighbourhood working, require time to bed in and lead to long-term change and improvement. Areas that have declined over a period of 30 years or more will take more than two or three years to turn around. Residents who have lived through the decline will take some time to be convinced that change is real and long-term.

Managing any mismatch between improved social and physical circumstances and decreased personal happiness is one of the key challenges for the initial and even medium-term period of any new ways of working. Identifying where these mismatches are, so that they can be addressed, is a key feature of evaluation. Organisations will need determination, commitment and resilience to hang on in there for the long term.

Disseminating and learning lessons

Evaluation is not an end in itself. It is only of use if it achieves better results. For this to happen, the findings should be disseminated within the organisation and its partners as well as further afield. This includes:

- Board members/local councillors
- Staff
- The local community
- Partner organisations and agencies
- Other similar programmes and projects
- Policy-makers, planners and politicians regionally (and nationally, if appropriate).

A creative approach to dissemination, using newsletters, posters, short films and presentations, will result in much more widespread and effective distribution of key messages.

Action evaluations

NORTH BENWELL NEIGHBOURHOOD MANAGEMENT PARTNERSHIP

NEWCASTLE UPON TYNE

The Neighbourhood Management Initiative (NMI) in North Benwell, Newcastle is led by Home Group, in partnership with Newcastle City Council, Bridging Newcastle/Gateshead Pathfinder and Northumbria Police.

An 18 month 'action evaluation' was carried out between 2004 and 2006, led by SRC. The lessons gained from the evaluation were put into practice as it progressed, to improve performance and learn from experience.

The evaluation had two main aims:

- To establish if the initiative was meeting its aims and objectives
- To test out whether it was meeting the aspirations of its key partners and beneficiaries (local people, service providers, funding and support agencies).

The first phase of the evaluation concentrated on:

- Measuring success against targets
- Enabling participants to identify evidence and reflect on it
- Provide accountability to partners, local people and funders.

→

This was achieved by:

- Producing a baseline report with statistics about the area
- Interviews with local stakeholders to gather perceptions on achievements and weaknesses
- A household survey of 200 residents in the neighbourhood (a quarter of whom had been interviewed in 2004) to gather quantitative information on awareness of the NMI and access to services
- A review of monitoring information produced by staff
- An interim report, recording the progress and achievements of the first 18 months of the initiative.

The second phase concentrated on providing evidence of what works, for whom and in what circumstances.

This was achieved by:

- An update of the household survey including attitude and behaviour statements to find out how people felt about living in the area
- Outreach sessions with young people and members of the BME community to assess the impact of the NMI on rarely-heard groups
- Interviews with the staff, key partners and local agencies to assess the impact of the NMI and the working relationships between partners
- Meeting observations to understand how NMI staff represent themselves to external agencies and how the aims and objectives were promoted to external agencies
- The development of good practice case studies to share learning
- A review of monitoring information
- A final report providing detailed information on how improvements in service delivery have been achieved.

As well as an evaluation report, NMI staff were also provided with a comprehensive toolkit to enable them to be self-evaluating in the future.

CHAPTER 8

LOOKING FORWARD

This final chapter looks to the future and what may be needed to make sure that our deprived neighbourhoods can be successful places to live and work in for the foreseeable future. It also looks briefly at what further changes housing providers could make to deliver the neighbourhood agenda more effectively.

To become and stay successful, deprived neighbourhoods need a holistic and consistent approach from policy-makers. Too often in the past, governments have veered from one form of intervention to another, ploughing in capital without revenue, then revenue without capital, focusing on local economic development for a time, then changing tack and concentrating on housing investment. Is it any wonder that neighbourhoods have not always responded as expected?

Lessons have, of course, been learned, but they have not always been translated into concerted, coordinated action on the ground. It is no coincidence that the best of the long-term neighbourhood intervention programmes (Housing Action Trusts and New Deal for Communities) have been holistic by design and community-based or led in their delivery.

The reality of neighbourhoods is inevitably complex, requiring an equally complex response. Tinkering with deprived neighbourhoods will not make or keep them successful. To achieve the long-term success of neighbourhoods it will be essential, at the very least, to get some of the basics right:

- Early and, if necessary, sustained action by key stakeholders to deal effectively with top community priorities – usually anti-social behaviour and environmental services
- Ongoing neighbourhood management – an active partnership between service providers and the community, with local staff in a local base
- Ongoing and regular investment in the local infrastructure and facilities
- Maintaining a stable or buoyant local economy and housing market

- Tackling local worklessness effectively
- A strong, empowered and cohesive community, with direct control over some neighbourhood assets, a stable revenue base and access to resources for strengthening or capacity building
- A supportive and enabling local authority
- Local councillors acting as community champions.

With these things in place, even the most difficult neighbourhoods have a good chance of becoming successful in the long term.

A wider role for housing associations

Housing associations are in pole position to deliver much of the neighbourhood agenda, but they need to be bold and further extend their role beyond housing provision. There is the opportunity to become social investment agencies and community anchors, using their increased freedom to operate outside their traditional housing provider boundaries, and taking, in many cases, a leading role in delivering successful neighbourhoods. Those with limited experience in this field need to learn about what works and what doesn't from those that have already made the change. Although housing provision will always be the core business for most of them, and a sound asset base is essential for the sustainability of wider activities, the days of associations acting solely as managers of social housing are fading fast.

Housing associations should also be much more proactive in their encouragement of community ownership and/or management of their assets. Their business plans should include provision for promoting the transfer of appropriate stock to neighbourhood bodies, where this would contribute to successful neighbourhoods, as well as deliver local housing objectives. Housing association staff should be promoting and supporting community management and asset transfer, not simply waiting for requests from their tenants. Capacity building will also be essential.

It remains to be seen how this shift fits in with the move to yet larger housing association groupings. One view is that the size of an association is irrelevant; it is how it delivers services in neighbourhoods that counts, and that it has a local presence. Nevertheless, there are legitimate concerns that the larger housing associations become, and despite their best intentions, the less in touch with neighbourhoods and their communities they will be. Should this happen, associations may begin to write themselves out of the neighbourhood agenda, just at the time when they should be writing themselves into it. There are clearly some difficult decisions ahead.

ALMOs – a new future for council housing?

Other housing providers, especially ALMOs, need to take an equally expansive view of their neighbourhood role. Local authority housing departments and ALMOs have the advantage of being owned and managed locally; their stock is focused on specific, often deprived, neighbourhoods where, unlike housing assocations, they are usually still the dominant owner.

ALMOs now manage about one million homes in England; most are already delivering good quality services for tenants, achieving 2 or 3 star ratings from the Audit Commission and are on target to deliver the government's Decent Homes Standard.

Despite their success, ALMOs are not necessarily here to stay; most have temporary contracts with local councils and could be wound up once decent homes work is complete. Many tenants and the ALMOs themselves would prefer to have a long-term future in reshaping the way council housing is run. To achieve that, local authority housing revenue accounts need to be put on a different financial basis.

ALMOs need to become more flexible and sustainable organisations, able to address the varied needs of the places and tenants they serve, and help contribute to wider local priorities. They need to work much more closely with other neighbourhood providers. ALMOs should be taking on wider physical and social regeneration initiatives on behalf of local authorities and other service providers and actively promoting tenant control of their stock in neighbourhoods where there is interest.

It is important to look beyond decent homes targets and look more closely at how estates are managed as part of an holistic approach to neighbourhoods, including how council housing can be integrated within wider neighbourhoods.

Towards the accountable neighbourhood

Some of the changes needed to create and sustain successful neighbourhoods have been put in place by government, but there is still a long way to go. The Local Government White Paper (2006) signalled a further move in the right direction, but stopped short of endorsing some key aspects of the neighbourhood agenda.

The concept of 'double devolution' – cascading power from central to local government and from local government to neighbourhoods – has less emphasis than might have been expected; community calls for action are to be channelled through local councillors, to strengthen their role and give a boost to local democracy; the regulatory framework on councils has been slimmed down. Widely canvassed proposals for a national neighbourhoods charter have been shelved.

There is much welcome reference in the White Paper to 'empowerment' and 'capacity building' as prerequisites for the driving up of service standards at neighbourhood level. Yet the mechanisms to achieve this are notable by their absence. Despite the resources ploughed into capacity building in recent years, it is an area that is still by and large poorly understood, under-resourced and badly delivered. It too often turns out to mean enabling rather than empowering.

The White Paper reiterates the long-established government view that the simplest and most direct way to increase people's control is to give them more choice. Many regeneration practitioners and residents would argue that *influence* is more important for those interested in taking more responsibility and exerting control. Rather than shopping around, it appears that what many people want are high quality, accessible and responsive services over which they have influence. But influence, how to achieve it in the right place, at the right time and at the right level, has to be learned. Residents (and many professionals) do not enter the neighbourhood arena equipped with the knowledge and skills they need to influence what happens there.

As a minimum, there is a need to:

- Provide guidance on capacity building: what is it, how do you do it, when, where and with whom
- Ensure there is high quality community development support in place (with training if necessary)
- Identify the appropriate intermediary bodies and ensure they are geared up (ie local agencies which can advise, support and mediate between communities and service providers)
- Resource neighbourhood groups and the community and voluntary sector, to enable them to carry out their role effectively
- Devise and apply light touch, creative and locally tailored monitoring and evaluation methods which involve residents.

Overall, the Local Government White Paper (2006) places more emphasis on encouragement and rather less on prescription and standard setting. It is certainly a step in the right direction, towards more empowered neighbourhoods and stronger communities, but it remains to be seen whether this encouragement will be enough to focus the attention of local authorities and others on the neighbourhood agenda. For those performing well and already delivering, further encouragement may well be enough; for others, there may yet be a role for the carrot and stick.

History suggests that most significant change only happens in neighbourhoods (and elsewhere) when encouragement is backed with resources and a clear strategic framework. Changes that may need to be considered in the future, to deliver successful neighbourhoods, might include:

- Extending the community call for action approach, where local authorities and other service providers are obliged to respond to requests from neighbourhoods for asset transfers to small, community-based organisations

- Introducing a community right to buy neighbourhood assets, along similar lines to that now available to local communities in Scotland

- Further encouragement for local authorities to transfer ownership of housing to community-led vehicles, particularly Community Gateway and Community Land Trusts

- Promotion of and support for tenant management for housing association tenants

- Looking again at the potential for neighbourhood mayors, working with an expanded network of parish councils, within the framework of a national neighbourhoods charter

- An expansion of the Neighbourhood Renewal Fund, due for review in 2007/2008, and the Single Community Programme, to continue and broaden the revenue channelled into priority neighbourhoods where strengthening of local communities is still needed

- Setting standards for all housing providers engaged in the neighbourhood agenda. The Cave Review of 2007 looks to significant changes in the way social housing is regulated, with scope for an increased role for residents. If neighbourhood management and community empowerment are to attract the level of investment and support needed from government, some degree of accountability – and by extension regulation – is inevitable and should be broadly welcomed. The Communities Standard for Housing Associations, under development by the Housing Corporation as part of its Neighbourhoods and Communities Strategy, needs to have teeth if it is to make a real contribution to successful neighbourhoods.

Changing cultures, changing places

The outlook for our deprived neighbourhoods is improving. We have learned some important lessons; we know what works and what does not; although there will never be enough resources to tackle all the problems, there is the prospect of LAAs ensuring more strategic use of the resources coming into a neighbourhood and therefore levering in more. Successful neighbourhoods are firmly on the political radar and there is every indication that this interest is likely to be sustained. There is much for housing providers and others to do.

Delivering the neighbourhood agenda successfully in years to come will, however, depend on setting these policy priorities within a changing social and cultural context. While most people now have more choice of goods and services than ever before, impersonal systems reduce the scope for a human dimension to service delivery. The increasing emphasis people now place on the local, the smaller scale, and on individualism is a rejection of the remote, the impersonal and the paternalism which still characterises much of the public and social sector.

The impact of this is felt nowhere more keenly than in unsuccessful neighbourhoods. Anti-social behaviour, dirty streets and graffiti result from the actions of some of the people who live there. They don't respect where they live, those in authority or the often remote structures which seem to have little relevance to their daily lives.

But this perceived lack of respect is found in successful neighbourhoods too, albeit in different forms; in fact, it is endemic. As a society we question the judgement of the police, the diagnosis of the doctor, the views of the teacher as never before. All of us are challenging, in one form or another, our relationship with neighbourhood service providers. The ability of these services to continue reforming themselves is crucially important for the neighbourhood agenda.

Those who live in deprived neighbourhoods need to change too. If we want to transform places, we have to empower people – not just individually, but also collectively. People need to use their growing individual power to work with others to strengthen their communities and help change the places where they live. Making and sustaining successful neighbourhoods requires a joint effort, and community accountability will be a key factor too.

It will be challenging, difficult and uncomfortable. Handing over power, creating self-determination, choice and control where it does not exist will cause a significant shake-down in the way things are done. Of course, not every individual wants to be challenging; not every community wants to be empowered. But we know from experience, that those that do can make a real difference, particularly where they are supported by organisations that have made significant cultural changes themselves.

CIH's 2001 good practice guide on neighbourhood management concluded that:

> *"A truly comprehensive ...approach to neighbourhood sustainability needs to bring together the local control of services and investment in renewal programmes.*

Putting local communities in the driving seat in this respect raises the possibility of community-generated neighbourhood development plans and frameworks and a specific focus on community-owned assets."

This message is as valid today as it was then; it holds the key to successful neighbourhoods. We need to give it our best shot if we are to turn round our most deprived places and make a better job of it than we have managed in the past.

APPENDIX A

REFERENCES AND SOURCES OF FURTHER INFORMATION

Books and reports

Allen, C et al (2005) *Mixed tenure 20 years on: nothing out of the ordinary* Chartered Institute of Housing for the Joseph Rowntree Foundation

Amas, N and Crosland, B (2006) *Understanding the stranger: building bridges community handbook* ICAR & Calouste Gulbenkian Foundation

Audit Commission (2005) *Governing partnerships: Bridging the accountability gap*

Audit Commission (1999) *Listen up! Effective community consultation*

Bailey, N, Haworth, A, Manzi, T, Paranagamage, P, and Roberts, M (2006) *Creating and Sustaining Mixed Income Communities*, Chartered Institute of Housing for the Joseph Rowntree Foundation

Berube, A (2005) *Mixed Communities in England: A US perspective on evidence and policy prospects*, Joseph Rowntree Foundation

Big Lottery Fund, *Investing in ideas for growing community assets*

Blackaby, B (2004) *Community Cohesion and Housing: A Good Practice Guide*, Chartered Institute of Housing and the Housing Corporation

Bowles, M and Pitchford, M (2006) *Communities and Leadership: a paper summarising discussion points at the CDF debate on 4 October 2005*, Community Development Foundation

Bound, K and Skidmore P (2005) *Mapping governance at the local level in England*, Joseph Rowntree Foundation

Burgess, P, Hall, S, Mawson, J, and Pearce G (2001) *Devolved approaches to local governance – Policy and practice in neighbourhood management*, Joseph Rowntree Foundation

Burwood, S (2006) *Local Government, New Localism and the Delivery of Regeneration: A BURA Steering and Development Forum Report*, BURA

Bury, F and Mulgan G (2006) *Double Devolution: the renewal of local government*, The Smith Institute

Cambridge Economic Associates (2006) *Using data to improve services: a toolkit for neighbourhood management initiatives*

Carley, M (2005) *Bringing 'neighbourhood' centre stage; a report on a 24 hour event for unitary authorities,* Joseph Rowntree Foundation and the ODPM Neighbourhood Renewal Unit

Clarke, R, Diacon, D, Guimaraes, S (2005) *Redefining the Commons: Locking in Value through Community Land Trusts*, Building and Social Housing Foundation

Communities and Local Government Department (CLG) (2007) *Ends and Means: The Future Roles of Social Housing in England* (the Hills Report)

Communities and Local Government Department (CLG) (2007) *Making Assets Work: The Quirk Review of Community Asset Management and Ownership*

Communities and Local Government Department (CLG) (2006) *Independent Review of Regulation of Social Housing: a call for evidence*

Communities and Local Government Department (CLG) (2006) *From Decent Homes to Sustainable Communities: A discussion paper*

Communities and Local Government Department (CLG) (2006) *A Decent Home: Definitions and guidance for implementation*

Communities and Local Government Department (CLG) (2006) *Respect Standard for Housing Management – A Guide for Landlords*

Communities and Local Government Department (CLG) (2006) *Review of Arms Length Housing Management Organisations*

Communities and Local Government Department (CLG) (2006) *Strong and Prosperous Communities: The Local Government White Paper*

Communities and Local Government Department (CLG) (2007) *Strong and Prosperous Communities – The Local Government White Paper Making it happen: Implementation Plan*

Cope, H (2004) *Social Capital: the regeneration activities of the G15 housing associations,* G15 Group

Craig, J and Skidmore P (2005) *How community organisations put citizens in the driving seat*, DEMOS

Crossley, R (2006) *Tenant Management: an example of a successful neighbourhood-based empowerment programme,* CLG Neighbourhood Renewal Unit

Crossley, R and Gaster, L (2000) *Community development: Making a difference in social housing*, Joseph Rowntree Foundation

Dawley, S, Conway, C and Charles, D (2005) *The dynamics of learning and knowledge within community-led urban regeneration: the Lower Ouseburn Valley,* Centre for Urban and Regional Development Studies (CURDS)

Department of Health and NHS (2006) *Our Health, Our Care, Our Say: a new direction for community services*

Duncan, P (2003), *Taking Control in Your Community: A guide for housing association tenants,* The Confederation of Co-operative Housing and the Housing Corporation

Duncan, P and Thomas, S (2001) *Neighbourhood Management: A Good Practice Guide*, Chartered Institute of Housing and the Housing Corporation

Duncan, P and Thomas, S (2000) *Neighbourhood Regeneration – Resourcing community involvement*, Joseph Rowntree Foundation

Evans, R and Meegan R (2006) *Up your street: Housing Associations and the neighbourhoods and communities agenda*, Liverpool John Moores University and the Housing Corporation

Gaventa, J (2004) *Representation, Community Leadership and Participation: Citizen Involvement in Neighbourhood Renewal and Local Governance,* Institute of Development Studies

Gilchrist, A (2004) *The Well-Connected Community: A networking approach to community development*, The Community Development Foundation

Green, A and Owen, D (2006) *The geography of poor skills and access to work*, Joseph Rowntree Foundation

Groves, R and Sankey, S (2005) *Implementing new powers for private sector housing renewal*, Joseph Rowntree Foundation

HACASChapman Hendy (2003) *Empowering Communities – the Community Gateway Model*, Chartered Institute of Housing

Hart, L (2005) *To have and to hold: The DTA guide to asset development for community and social enterprise*, Development Trust Association

Hilder, P (2005) *Seeing the wood for the trees: the evolving landscape for neighbourhood arrangements,* The Young Foundation

Hilder, P and James, S (2006) *Transforming Neighbourhoods – Neighbourhood Policy: the rationale, the approach and the emergency menu of options,* The Young Foundation

Hilder, P and James, S (2006) *Tools and Processes for Neighbourhood Problem-Solving: the place for charters, inquiries and community initiatives in new neighbourhood arrangements,* The Young Foundation

HM Home Office Civil Renewal Unit (2005) *Together We Can: People and Government, working together to make life better*

HM Home Office Task Force (2006) *Respect Action Plan*

HM Treasury and Office of the Deputy Prime Minister (2006) *Devolving Decision Making: Meeting the regional economic challenge: The importance of cities to regional growth*

Home Office (2004) White Paper, *Building Communities, Beating Crime*, Home Office

Housing Corporation (2006) *Neighbourhoods and Communities Strategy*

Housing Corporation (2006) *Review of regulatory and compliance requirements for RSLs. A report to the Housing Corporation by a review group chaired by Sir Les Elton*

Independent Commission of Inquiry into Council Housing (2002) *One size doesn't fit all: community housing and flourishing neighbourhoods*

Janis Dean Associates (2006) *Rationalisation of Housing Association Stock: Review Paper,* Chartered Institute of Housing and the Housing Corporation

Joseph Rowntree Foundation (2006) *Foundations: Mixed Communities – Success and Sustainability*

Joseph Rowntree Charitable Trust and Joseph Rowntree Reform Trust (2006) *Power to the People*, Power Inquiry

Joseph Rowntree Foundation (2007) *Changing Neighbourhoods: Lessons from the JRF Neighbourhood Programme*

Jupp, B (1999) *Living Together – Community Life on Mixed Tenure Estates*, DEMOS

Katz, B (2004) *Neighbourhoods of choice and connection: The evolution of American neighbourhood policy and what it means for the United Kingdom,* Joseph Rowntree Foundation

Leadbeater, C (2004) *Personalisation through participation: A new script for public services*, DEMOS

Lister, S, Perry, J and Thornley, M (2007) *Community Engagement in Housing-Led Regeneration,* Chartered Institute of Housing and TPAS

Local Government Association (LGA) (2004) *Independence, Opportunity, Trust: a manifesto for local government. Towards self-governing communities: the role of local government in civil renewal*

Local Government Association (LGA) (2004) *Making decisions locally*

Local Government Association (LGA) (2005) *The next four years – the future is local*

Local Government Association (LGA) (2006) *Closer to people and places: a new vision for local government*

London School of Economics (2006) *One size still doesn't fit all: final report of the independent commission of inquiry into the future of council housing in Birmingham*

Lyons Inquiry into Local Government (2006) *National prosperity, local choice and civic engagement* HM Treasury

Lyons Report on Local Government Finance (2007) Communities and Local Government Department

Moran, D, Root, A, Smith, M, and Sullivan H (2001) *Area Committees and Neighbourhood Management*, Local Government Information Unit

Mulgan, G and Bury, F (2006) *Double devolution: the renewal of local government,* The Smith Institute

National Housing Federation (2003) *Annual Conference report*

National Housing Federation (2006) *Tenant Involvement Commission: report of written submissions*

National Neighbourhood Management Network (2005) *Delivering neighbourhood management: a practical guide*

National Neighbourhood Management Network (2006) *The case for neighbourhood management: how to get communities involved in local decisions*

Newman, I (2005) *Parish and town councils and neighbourhood governance,* Joseph Rowntree Foundation

Office of the Deputy Prime Minister (ODPM) (2006) *Communities Taking Control: Final Report of the Cross-sector Work Group on Community Ownership and Management of Assets*

Office of the Deputy Prime Minister (ODPM) (2006) *Empowerment and the Deal for Devolution*

Office of the Deputy Prime Minister (ODPM) (2005) *How to manage residential areas*

Office of the Deputy Prime Minister (ODPM) (2005) *Making it happen in neighbourhoods. The national strategy for neighbourhood renewal – four years on*

Office of the Deputy Prime Minister (ODPM) (2005) *Neighbourhood Management – working together to create Cleaner Safer Greener Communities*

Office of the Deputy Prime Minister (ODPM) (2005) *New Localism – Citizen Engagement, Neighbourhoods and Public Services: Evidence from Local Government*

Office of the Deputy Prime Minister (ODPM) (2006) *Research Report 2: Data Provision for Neighbourhood Renewal – Final Report*

Office of the Deputy Prime Minister (ODPM) (2005) *Research Report 16: Improving delivery of mainstream services in deprived areas – the role of community involvement*

Office of the Deputy Prime Minister (ODPM) (2005) *Research Report 17: New Deal for Communities 2001-2005 An Interim Evaluation*

Office of the Deputy Prime Minister (ODPM) (2005) *Research Report 19: Seeking the Lessons: an evaluation of the Neighbourhood Renewal Unit's Skills and Knowledge Programme*

Office of the Deputy Prime Minister (ODPM) (2006) *Research Report 22: National Evaluation of Single Local Management Centres*

Office of the Deputy Prime Minister (ODPM) (2006) *Research Report 25: Rolling Out Neighbourhood Management: A Theme Report from the Pathfinder Programme National Evaluation*

Office of the Deputy Prime Minister (ODPM) (2006) *Research Report 26: Neighbourhood Management Pathfinder Programme Baseline Report – Summary*

Office of the Deputy Prime Minister (ODPM) (2006) *Research Report 27: Alternative Approaches to Neighbourhood Management: 7 Case Study Summaries and Analysis National Evaluation of the Neighbourhood Management Pathfinder Programme*

Office of the Deputy Prime Minister (ODPM) (2004) *Neighbourhood Management Pathfinder Programme National Evaluation – Annual Review 2002/03 Research Report*

Office of the Deputy Prime Minister (ODPM) (2004) *Neighbourhood Management Pathfinder Programme National Evaluation – Annual Review 2003/04 Key Findings*

Office of the Deputy Prime Minister (ODPM) (2005) *The Safer and Stronger Communities Fund*

Office of the Deputy Prime Minister (ODPM) (2006) *All Our Futures: The challenges for local governance in 2015*

Office of the Deputy Prime Minister (ODPM) (2006) *Alternative Approaches to Neighbourhood Management: 6 Full Case Studies: National Evaluation of the Neighbourhood Management Pathfinder Programme*

Office of the Deputy Prime Minister (ODPM) (2005) *Vibrant Local Leadership*

Office of the Deputy Prime Minister (ODPM) (2006) *The National Neighbourhood Management Network: Membership information leaflet*

Office of the Deputy Prime Minister (ODPM) (2006) *State of English Cities: Urban Research Summary 21*

Office of the Deputy Prime Minister (ODPM) (2004) *Local Area Agreements: a prospectus*

Office of the Deputy Prime Minister and the Department for Transport (2006) *National Evaluation of Local Strategic Partnerships: Formative Evaluation and Action Research Programme 2002-2005 – Executive Summary to Final Report*

Office of the Deputy Prime Minister (ODPM) and Home Office (2004) *Citizen Engagement and Public Services: Why Neighbourhoods Matter*

Page, D (2006) *Respect and Renewal: a study of neighbourhood social regeneration,* Joseph Rowntree Foundation

Paskell, C and Power, A (2005) *'The future's changed': Local impacts of housing, environment and regeneration policy since 1997,* Centre for Analysis of Social Exclusion

Power, A (1999) *Neighbourhood Management,* London School of Economics

Power, A (2004) *Neighbourhood Management and the Future of Urban Areas,* London School of Economics

Power, A (2006) *The changing face of cities; environment on the edge,* United Nations Environment Programme

Proctor, K (2000) *Community-Led Estate Regeneration Handbook,* Churches National Housing Coalition and the Housing Corporation

Randle, A (2005) *Councils embracing localism: lessons in decentralisation from Birmingham, Wakefield and West Sussex,* New Local Government Network

RENEW Northwest (2006) *Making a difference – Participation and Wellbeing,* New Start Publishing Ltd

Robinson, D, Coward, S, Fordham, T, Green, S and Reeve K (2004) *How Housing Management can Contribute to Community Cohesion: A Research Report,* Chartered Institute of Housing

Robinson, F, Shaw, K and Davidson, G (2005) *'On the side of the angels': community involvement in the governance of neighbourhood renewal,* Taylor and Francis Journals

Rogers, R (2005) *Towards a Strong Urban Renaissance*, Urban Task Force

Rowe, S and Zitron, J (2002) *Beyond Bricks and Mortar: bringing regeneration into stock transfer,* Chartered Institute of Housing

Rowlands, R, Murie, A and Tice, A (2006) *More than tenure mix: developer and purchaser attitudes to new housing estates,* Chartered Institute of Housing for the Joseph Rowntree Foundation

Shared Intelligence (2005) *New Deal for Communities Succession Strategies*, ODPM Neighbourhood Renewal Unit

Silverman, E, Lupton, R and Fenton, A (2005) *A Good Place for Children? Attracting and Retaining Families in Inner Urban Mixed Income Communities*, Chartered Institute of Housing for the Joseph Rowntree Foundation

Skidmore, P, Bound, K, Lownsbrough, H (2006) *Community Participation – who benefits?* DEMOS/Joseph Rowntree Foundation

Social Regeneration Consultants (SRC) (2003) *Delivering Neighbourhood Management: A Final Report for Hartlepool New Deal for Communities*

Social Regeneration Consultants (SRC) (2004) *Neighbourhood Management in Hyndburn: Interim and Final Reports*

Social Regeneration Consultants (SRC) (2006) *North Benwell Neighbourhood Management Initiative: Partnership Development Toolkit*

Stoker, G (2004) *New Localism: The argument for decentralisation gains ground in England*, Institute for Political and Economic Governance

Taylor, M and Wilson, M (2006) *The importance of the neighbourhood: Tackling the implementation gap*, Joseph Rowntree Foundation

Taylor, M, Wilson, M, Wilde, P and Purdue, D (2005) *Lending a hand: The value of 'light touch' support in empowering communities,* Joseph Rowntree Foundation

Taylor, M, Wilson, M, Wilde, P and Purdue, D (2005) *Evaluating community projects: a practical guide,* Joseph Rowntree Foundation

Taylor, M (2000) *Top down meets bottom up: Neighbourhood Management,* Joseph Rowntree Foundation

Terry, R, Doolittle, I and Perry, J (2005) *ALMOs – a new future for council housing,* Chartered Institute of Housing

The Association of Community Workers and Community Work Training Co. (2001) *Community Work Skills Manual*

The Bridge Group (2003) *Growing confidence: introducing the community gateway model,* Chartered Institute of Housing

The Empty Homes Agency (2005) *Low Demand Policy Statement*

Tunstall, R and Coulter, A (2006) *Twenty-five years on twenty estates,* Joseph Rowntree Foundation

Tunstall, R and Fenton, A (2006) *In the Mix: A review of mixed income, mixed tenure and mixed communities,* Housing Corporation, Joseph Rowntree Foundation, English Partnerships

Wadhams, C (2006) *An Opportunity waiting to happen: Housing Associations as 'Community Anchors',* Hact and National Housing Federation

Wadhams, C (2002) *Quality Neighbourhoods: A Guide to Neighbourhood Management for Registered Social Landlords,* Chris Wadhams Associates and Harding Housing Association

Young Foundation (2006) *Transforming Neighbourhoods: tools and processes for neighbourhood problem-solving*

Websites and online resources

Balsall Heath Forum, *Vibrant Villages: Building quality of lives in quality neighbourhoods* www.balsallheath forum.org.uk/Books_and_Papers.htm

Chartered Institute of Housing, *Empowering Communities – the Community Gateway Model* – Progress bulletins at: www.cih.org/gateway

Chartered Institute of Housing (2007) *Delivering Efficiency: Resident-led self-regulation: potential and prospects* www.cih.org/policy/resident-led-self-regulation.pdf

Chartered Institute of Housing (2007) *The Rationalisation of Housing Association Stock* www.cih.org/policy/RationalisationOfStock.pdf

Confederation for Co-operative Housing *Taking control in your neighbourhood* *www.communitiestakingcontrol.org*

Housing Corporation (2007) *The rationalisation of housing association stock – a guide and toolkit* www.housingcorp.gov.uk/publications

Joseph Rowntree Foundation summaries below – access via www.jrf.org.uk/knowledge/findings and input report number

Joseph Rowntree Foundation (2003) *Neighbourhoods that work* 733

Joseph Rowntree Foundation (1999) *Social cohesion and urban inclusion for disadvantaged neighbourhoods* 4109

Joseph Rowntree Foundation (2005) *Transatlantic perspectives on mixed communities* 0295

Joseph Rowntree Foundation (2005) *Economic segregation in England: causes, consequences and policy* 0645

Joseph Rowntree Foundation (1999) *The problem of low demand in inner city areas* 519

Joseph Rowntree Foundation (2006) *Developer and purchaser attitudes to new-build mixed tenure housing* 0126

Joseph Rowntree Foundation (2005) *Monitoring poverty and social exclusion in the UK* 0665

Joseph Rowntree Foundation (2005) *Environmental problems and service provision in deprived and more affluent neighbourhoods* 0515

Joseph Rowntree Foundation (2005) *Sustainable neighbourhoods: the role of housing markets and community assets* 0145

Joseph Rowntree Foundation (2002) *Community governance for mixed tenure neighbourhoods* n102

Joseph Rowntree Foundation (2005) *Messages from three mixed-tenure communities* 0465

Joseph Rowntree Foundation (2005) *Effective participation in anti-poverty and regeneration work and research* 0395

Joseph Rowntree Foundation (1995) *The effect of community regeneration organisations on neighbourhood regeneration* H10

Joseph Rowntree Foundation (2006) *The value added by community involvement in governance* 0406

Office of the Deputy Prime Minister (ODPM) (2005) *What is a sustainable Community?* www.communities.gov.uk/index.asp?id=1139866

Paul Hilder (2006) *The true value of neighbourhood arrangements*, The Young Foundation www.youngfoundation.org.uk/index.php?p=303

Home Office (2006) Police and Justice Bill, http://police.homeoffice.gov.uk/police-reform/PoliceandJusticeBill/

The Young Foundation, *Double devolution: the renewal of local government,* www.youngfoundation.org.uk/?p=290

APPENDIX B

GLOSSARY

ALMO
A company owned by a local authority, but operating under a management agreement between the local authority and the ALMO in order to manage and improve council housing stock.

Community Land Trusts
A mechanism for the democratic ownership of land by a local community which uses the increasing value of land for community rather than commercial benefit.

Community Gateway
A new and innovative way of running social housing. Tenants and leaseholders have a greater influence over how a housing association or stock transfer organisation is run, with involvement at a wide variety of levels, including being active board members.

Decent Homes Standard
The minimum standard for social housing, set by government. A decent home is one that is wind and weather tight, warm and has modern facilities. All social housing in England should meet this standard by 2010.

Devolution
Transferring some of the power and responsibilities from central government to regional bodies, local government and neighbourhood communities.

Gershon
Sir Peter Gershon's review of public sector efficiency for the Treasury, published in 2004. It focused on moving resources to 'front-line' services.

Guide Neighbourhoods Programme
A CLG-led programme to enable strong, successful resident-led neighbourhood organisations to share their knowledge and experience with other neighbourhoods trying to tackle similar problems. There are currently 15 Guide Neighbourhoods.

Housing market renewal pathfinders (HMR)

9 Pathfinder programmes have been established in the midlands and north of England in areas experiencing low demand housing. The pathfinders bring together local authorities and key agencies to develop 10-15 year strategic plans to boost demand and create sustainable neighbourhoods.

Local Area Agreements (LAA)

Funding agreements between central and local government in a local area. Their aim is to achieve local solutions that meet local needs, while also contributing to national priorities and the achievement of standards set by central government.

Local Public Service Agreements

Voluntary agreements between the government and an individual local authority. Under the agreement, a council agrees to a number of targets and sets out how it will improve local public services. In return, the government sets out how it will reward those improvements.

Local Strategic Partnerships (LSP)

Partnerships to improve quality of life by coordinating local service delivery more effectively and by involving all sectors of society: public, private, community and voluntary. LSPs are optional, although required for some local authorities in order to receive neighbourhood renewal funding.

Mainstreaming

Rolling out neighbourhood management across a local authority area, beyond initial pilot projects.

Modernisation agenda

The government's strategy to reform and update local government.

Neighbourhood management

A process which enables local communities to work with providers of neighbourhood services to meet local needs and expectations more effectively and in a way which secures and develops local accountability.

Respect agenda

Respect is about central government, local agencies, local communities and citizens working together to build a society in which people can respect one another – where anti-social behaviour is rare and tackled effectively, and communities can live in peace together.

Safer and Stronger Communities Fund
The Safer and Stronger Communities Fund was introduced for all local authorities in England in April 2005. The funding brings together CLG and Home Office funding streams aimed at tackling crime, ASB and drugs, empowering communities and improving the condition of streets and public spaces.

Single pot
Regeneration funds available from government, brought together through regional development agencies

Social capital
Social capital describes the pattern and intensity of networks among people and the shared values which arise from those networks. This includes aspects of citizenship, neighbourliness, trust and shared values, community involvement, volunteering, social networks and civic participation.

Special Purpose Vehicle/Joint venture Company
A partnership organisation established to deliver a programme of work – typically a major regeneration programme – which individual partners cannot deliver alone.

Super Output Areas (SOA)
SOAs are used by the Office for National Statistics Office for the collection and publication of small area statistics.

The Northern Way
A growth strategy set out in an ODPM 2004 report, *Moving Forward: The Northern Way*. Over the next 25 years the strategy aims to close the £30 million output gap between the north and the rest of England. It seeks to transform the north into an area with a world-class economy and outstanding quality of life.

APPENDIX C

TOGETHER WE CAN
GUIDE NEIGHBOURHOODS

The Guide Neighbourhoods programme was established to enable strong, successful resident-led neighbourhood organisations to share their knowledge and experience with other neighbourhoods trying to tackle similar problems.

The Guide Neighbourhoods are:

Balsall Heath Forum, Birmingham

Burrowes Street Tenant Management Organisation Ltd, Walsall

Castle Vale Community Housing Association, Birmingham

Eldonians Initiative, Liverpool

Goodwin Development Trust Ltd, Hull

Include Centre for Neighbourhood Management, Liverpool

Leicester North West Community Forum, Leicester

National Federation of Tenant Management Organisations, UK-wide

Neighbours4U, Kent

Pembroke Street Estate Management Board, Plymouth

Poplar Harca, London

Royds Community Association, Bradford

Seedley and Langworthy Trust, Salford

Stubbin Neighbourhood Association, Sheffield

Witton Lodge Community Association, Birmingham

Further information on the Guide Neighbourhoods programme, including contact details for each project, is available at www.housingjustice.org.uk/gn